Demystifying Economic Markets and Prices

Demystifying Economic Markets and Prices

Understanding Patterns and Practices in Everyday Life

Gregory R. Woirol

 PRAEGER®

An Imprint of ABC-CLIO, LLC
Santa Barbara, California • Denver, Colorado

Library of Congress Cataloging-in-Publication Data

Names: Woirol, Gregory R. (Gregory Ray), 1948– author.
Title: Demystifying economic markets and prices : understanding patterns and
    practices in everyday life / Gregory R. Woirol.
Description: Santa Barbara, California : Praeger, [2019] | Includes
    bibliographical references and index.
Identifiers: LCCN 2019016899 (print) | LCCN 2019018771 (ebook) |
    ISBN 9781440872532 (ebook) | ISBN 9781440872525 (hard copy : alk. paper)
Subjects: LCSH: Prices. | Supply and demand. | Markets. | Consumption
    (Economics)
Classification: LCC HB221 (ebook) | LCC HB221 .W64 2019 (print) |
    DDC 338.4/3—dc23
LC record available at https://lccn.loc.gov/2019016899

ISBN: 978-1-4408-7252-5 (print)
        978-1-4408-7253-2 (ebook)

23 22 21 20 19   1 2 3 4 5

This book is also available as an eBook.

Praeger
An Imprint of ABC-CLIO, LLC

ABC-CLIO, LLC
147 Castilian Drive
Santa Barbara, California 93117
www.abc-clio.com

This book is printed on acid-free paper ∞

Manufactured in the United States of America

For Susan, Samantha,
and Stephanie

Contents

Acknowledgments

The topics in this book were developed through conversations with many students and colleagues. I would like to thank them all, especially my colleagues Steve Overturf, Chuck Laine, Kim Thomas, Geetha Rajaram, Simon Lamar, and Roger White for their constant encouragement and for creating an engaging environment for thought and discussion.

I called upon the editorial and organizational skills of Maureen Nerio many times in writing this book, as well as the research assistance of the librarians at Whittier College. Knowing I could rely on them whenever needed made the tasks involved in research and writing easy and enjoyable.

I would especially like to thank Rick Sadler, Kim Thomas, and Paul Thomas for comments on various chapters in the book. I greatly appreciate the time and interest they gave to my requests for suggestions and criticisms. The book is clearly better for their advice.

My editors and production team at Praeger, including Hilary Claggett, Vince Burns, Kevin Downing, and Nicole Azze, provided the professional and personal assistance that any author could wish. Thank you for making the experience both pleasant and productive.

None of this could have be done without the loving support and encouragement of my wife, Sue, and my daughters, Samantha and Stephanie. *Triad mirabilis*, they make every day a miracle.

Introduction

Markets and Prices in Everyday Life

All living things develop ways to produce and consume what is needed to survive, yet as far as I know only humans use markets and prices as a way to do this. I expect that you spend a good part of most days dealing with markets and prices, but I am just as certain that the bumblebees, robins, and maple trees outside your window do not devote a speck of energy to the task. As a result, we are constantly dealing with issues that markets create. In a typical day you may wonder why your favorite candy bar varies so much in price between the vending machine down the hall and the local grocery warehouse, why your new car lost more than 10 percent of its value the instant it was driven off the lot, and why your home team superstar is paid extraordinarily more than less talented peers. The reason we choose to take on the issues created by markets and prices actually seems to be a simple one, and a good way to see it is to think about that purest of all contemporary American markets, the weekend yard sale.

Imagine it is a beautiful Saturday and your neighbor has told you that she is going to have a yard sale that day. She has cleaned out her garage and closets, dragged her old treasures to the driveway, and put tempting prices on the items for passersby to sort through. You decide to take advantage of her planning and effort and to put a few items of your own out on your front lawn. It gives you a chance to sort through the dross in that hall closet you haven't dared look into for the past five years and create some much needed storage space.

While setting your things out, you, of course, go see what your neighbor has to offer, and she takes a look at your offerings as well. Assume you see a set of four books she has put out for sale that you would really like to read.

You go over and ask if she is willing to trade something that you have for her books. She notices that old TV you had in your first apartment that would just fit a niche she has in her house, and offers the books for the TV. You say okay, and the deal is done.

This is a market in its most basic form, a trade of one good for another. Now, why do we do such a thing? The answer, of course, is obvious. We do it because we both gain from the trade. You got rid of that old TV that just took up space and received a set of books you would greatly enjoy reading. Your neighbor got rid of the old books she didn't care about and got in return a TV she could put to good use. In his book titled *The World Until Yesterday* about human life before the modern age, Jared Diamond points out that evidence of such trades dates back tens of thousands of years. According to Diamond, "Cro-Magnon sites in the interior of Pleistocene Europe contain Baltic marine amber and Mediterranean seashells transported a thousand miles inland, plus obsidian, flint, jasper, and other hard stones especially suitable for stone-tool-making and transported hundreds of miles from the sites where they had been quarried."

The value of markets in this way is easily demonstrated in the classroom when I bring a box of yard sale items from home, dump it out on a table, and ask students if they want to trade for any of my one-time treasures. Some offers I accept, and some I don't (an offer of a nice pen in trade is okay, but I have no use for chewing gum). After the deals are done and I ask the students who gained from the trades, their answers are immediate and clear. Both sides gain from voluntary trade between individuals.

If you think about it for a minute, this is a kind of economic magic. There are no more goods existing in the world, but after the trade there is more human satisfaction. Doing the trade is not costless, of course. You have to spend the time and energy to connect with another person and make the deal. But the outcome makes the effort worthwhile. Before the trade, there are X goods and Y satisfaction in the world, but after the trade there are still X goods, but now there is Y + Z satisfaction. Markets exist because of the Z added from trading one good for another.

So the basic reason for the existence of markets seems clear. But note that this is a very human thing. There is something in the way we function as living beings in evaluating objects that makes trading and markets a common human practice. It seems to be a part of the way that we think and behave in our contacts with what exists in the world and with each other. And note as well that the mutual gains from trade are only clear and straightforward when they are voluntary transactions between individuals. No one would argue that a compulsory trade of work for food between a slave and master creates mutually satisfying outcomes. And even in voluntary trades as soon as more than one person is involved on each side, then issues arise about the distribution of the gains from the transaction. To see this, assume in the yard sale trade with your neighbor that the books and TV you and your neighbor traded are the property of your domestic partners. The same gains from the trade will exist, but what do the partners get? How do they share in the gains? Because of the multiple parties involved, an enduring issue about trade deals between nations is that while overall each country gains, the gains are not distributed evenly and some people may lose.

Despite issues created by compulsion and multiple participants, the gains from trades are so evident and so strong that we choose to make transactions like this almost every day of our lives. According to World Bank data, China, from 1960 to 1980 under a system of rigidly controlled markets and almost no international trade, saw its real gross national product per capita double, while over the next thirty-five years from 1980 to 2015 under a system of much freer markets and much more open international trade the increase was forty-one times.

If that's what freer markets and trade can do for us, what about prices? The answer here again seems to be quite simple. Think again about your Saturday yard sale. Your neighbor, as you recall, put prices on all the items she put out on her driveway. You conveniently had a TV you could trade directly for her books, but clearly not every passerby is going to have an item to trade that your neighbor would be interested in. The way people have come up with to get around the problem of finding acceptable bartering transactions is to use money as an intermediate good. In general, your neighbor is going to trade her yard sale goods for money and then use the money to buy others things elsewhere that she wants.

The creation and use of money in this way is also an ancient human tradition. According to David Graeber in his book *Debt: The First 5,000 Years*, the concept of money dates in written records to Mesopotamian civilization around 3500 BCE. In human history, multitudes of things have been used as money, including tobacco, seashells, pieces of rock, gold, silver, pieces of paper, plastic, and electronic computer entries. The best things to use as money, and how to control its amount and quality, have been discovered by a long and often painful process of trial and error. But the basic use and value of money as an intermediate good in making trading easier is so clear that it has overcome all obstacles. There is no serious possibility that people will soon give up its use.

The gains from trade and the convenience of money explain much about why markets and prices exist, but they are not all that is going on. The gains from trade and the use of money create the possibility of another basic element that also seems to matter, and that is gains from specialization in producing things. This is another human practice that goes back to our very beginnings. Even the most simple of human societies that people have been able to observe tend to divide up the tasks of individual responsibilities. The reason is very practical. By specialization, people can get more of what they want from the resources in the world surrounding them. The gains from specialization seem to be so profound that it is not even a practice unique to human beings. Individual ants and honeybees certainly have specific tasks that they perform, and many other animals divide up the chores of raising offspring or hunting for food. At an even more fundamental level, individual cells specialize in multicellular living things. The most basic forms of life have single cells, and it is only after cells joined together and specialized in function that the complexity of the life that we know was created.

Specialization, then, seems to be central to the biology of successful living on earth. What specialization by people in producing things creates is, in effect, a second kind of economic magic. From exactly the same quantity of resources surrounding us, through specialization we can get more of the things we need. When Adam Smith wrote the first great book in economics, he emphasized the division of labor as a central cause of *The Wealth of Nations*. In Smith's example, ten workers specializing and dividing the work in a pin factory could produce about 48,000 pins a day, but "if they had all wrought separately and independently, and without any of them having been educated to this peculiar business, they certainly could not each of them have made twenty, perhaps not one pin in a day." Just like trade can create more satisfaction from the same amount of goods, specialization can create more goods from the same amount of resources.

Even better, the gains from trade and the gains from specialization are intimately linked. The possibilities from trade create more opportunities for specialization, and more specialization creates more possibilities for trade. It is because of the gains possible from specialization that we attach importance to such concepts as the division of labor, tools, machines, learning, education, innovation, invention, productivity, and technological change.

The gains from specialization and trade plus the convenience of money seem to be enough to explain why markets and prices exist in human societies, but there seems to be something more that is needed to explain the fact that the use of markets and prices have allowed human societies to grow. Specialization and trade would seem to be quite compatible with the existence of small-scale, stable, static human groups. But human societies using markets and prices tend to grow. What is going on here?

The answer to this question may lie in the results of another classroom demonstration that is easy to do. In this one, I divide students into two equal groups and ask one group to leave the room for a few minutes. I then unpack a box of coffee mugs and spread them out on a table in front of the remaining group. The students in the room are asked to line up in front of the class, take a coffee mug of their choice from the selection offered, and return to their seats with the cups. They are then asked to write on a piece of paper the dollar amount they would be willing to pay to buy their coffee mug. After turning in the slips of paper and returning the mugs to the table, the group then leaves the classroom and tells the other group to come in. When the second group comes in, I tell them in exactly the same way to line up, select a coffee mug, and return to their seats. They are then told that the coffee cup is theirs to keep. Once it is clear to everyone that they own the mug, they are asked to write on a slip of paper the dollar amount that they would be willing to sell the mug for. I then collect the paper slips and have the group in the hall return.

Every time I have done this activity, a comparison of the willing-to-pay prices to the willing-to-sell prices shows the average for the willing-to-sell price to be significantly higher. Now this seems to be a strange thing. The coffee mugs are exactly the same in the two cases. Admittedly the two groups of students are different, and the people involved are all college-aged and educated so they are not average folk, but the results are the same over and over again. The simple fact of ownership seems to make people value a good more.

I'm not sure where this comes from. Perhaps there is some basic biological factor at work. Many animals store, collect, or hoard food items for very understandable reasons related to their survival, so this reaction to living in our physical world may have deep roots. But people do not have to act this way. Certainly, many people choose to live their lives in ways where they share with others much or most of what they own or produce. Pastors and priests come to mind, as do volunteer social workers, Habitat for Humanity home builders, successful private sector business people who take low-paid public positions, and philanthropic billionaires. Whole societies can be organized on these principles. When Tony Horwitz wrote a book about his adventures following Captain James Cook's travels through the South Pacific, he talked with people who told stories about the old way of life in their world. As a native Australian put it, "life was important, the land was sacred, but not things and not surplus. If we went fishing and hunting and got more than we needed, we gave it away."

Despite these exceptions, the extra value put on personally owned goods seems to be a common human behavior. As an article on the rise and success of self-storage firms in the United States put it, "for some reason [people] seldom chuck any of this rubbish out." Ownership seems to be important to people, and the drive to acquire and accumulate that comes from putting value on ownership seems to be central in economic growth. Because of the value we place on ownership, we pay a great deal of attention to concepts that relate to property, from private versus public property rules, to property rights and property laws, taxes, inheritance laws, and privacy rules.

In the end, it doesn't matter if valuing things more because they are owned is fundamentally biological or social. Overall, it seems that people do place value on ownership, and this factor seems to be an important element in explaining why the gains from specialization and trade can lead to economic growth.

Markets and prices thus have good reasons to exist. They create the possibility for us to get more of what we need and want from the resources that surround us. If all this seems so commonplace that it is hardly worth mentioning, just reflect for a minute on ways today that we use invisible waves in the air around us. This is a resource that many of us find absolutely central to our current lives, yet it is a resource that people knew almost nothing about how to use not long ago. I expect it would be very difficult to tell the story of the discovery and development of radio, TV, cell phones, satellite communication, and the other goods that use these airwaves without talking about markets and prices.

The fact that markets and prices seem to be an important and distinctive way for humans to connect themselves to each other leads to another background point. That is that the patterns and practices we see in the prices and markets around us are not set in stone. If prices and markets do not work well, they can be changed. Economic laws are not like the laws of physics. As far as we have been able to discover, the patterns and relationships we see in physics are immutable. Gravity is a fact, energy exists, and matter responds to force. We have to take the laws of physics as they are and work with them as we go about our daily lives. This is not true, however, about economics. The patterns and practices we see in the prices and markets around us are all human creations. As a result, they can be modified at will. The ways that the patterns we see in prices and markets are controlled, changed, or even canceled are all about politics and government. The field of economics, as you may know, used to be called political economy, and an important perspective was lost when the name was changed. Mainstream economics as it is practiced today is about finding the best way to solve a problem, where best is defined in terms of the long-run use of resources. Political economy, on the other hand, is about what is possible. The contrast was neatly made in a January 2017 issue of *The Economist* magazine where one article, in light of the 2016 U.S. presidential election, criticized current economics for focusing on best solutions and not paying enough attention to what was politically possible, and the immediately following article presented the best solution for updating regional electric power grids and lamented that politics stopped its implementation.

What this all means is that if prices and markets are not working well, something can be done about it. It also means that the way that markets and prices work today is very much dependent on the social and political framework that exists today. The way that prices and markets worked in the U.S. economy in 1943 at the peak of World War II, for example, was not the same way they worked five years before in 1938, before the war began. And the way that prices and markets worked in East Germany in 1993 was not the same way as they worked in 1988, before the Berlin Wall fell.

All of these points provide a perspective on common economic practices and institutions that surround us, but I expect that they are not reflections that come to many peoples' minds as they go about their daily lives. We don't spend much time during a typical day thinking about why markets and prices exist because all our attention is taken up just in dealing with them. Living in a modern economy, what we know and care about is that our daily lives are deeply embedded in a matrix of markets and prices, that the realities of markets and prices are here to stay, and that dealing well with them can be a challenge. Some markets and prices we find easy to understand and don't cause us many problems, like the Saturday yard sale where you can trade your old TV for your neighbor's books. Some patterns in prices and markets also seem clear and self-evident, like the tendency for Halloween candy to be marked down in price the day after October 31 or the fact that our standard of living depends on the incomes we receive compared to the prices we pay for things. But other markets and prices work in ways that seem to be more mysterious, exasperating, frustrating, irritating, or even unfair.

The purpose of the following chapters is to discuss some of the patterns and practices we see in prices and markets that we commonly encounter in daily life in an economy like the American economy. Along the way, we will see why identical candy bars can vary so widely in price, why new cars lose value as soon as they are used cars, and why superstars can earn so much. This seems to be a task well worth undertaking, because deep down we understand the fundamental issues at stake. We know that if poorly managed the institutions and practices of prices and markets possess, at one extreme, the potential to disrupt our lives, destroy our standard of living, and even bring a nation to the edge of revolt. If you doubt this is true, just review the history of Venezuela in the 2010s. Yet if run well, at the other extreme, the use of prices and markets has the potential to create as yet undreamed of well-being, comfort, and human satisfaction. The challenge every society faces in using prices and markets is to avoid the bad effects and create the good. One way to start to face this challenge is to have a better understanding of prices and markets that we encounter in our daily lives.

CHAPTER ONE

Candy Bars, Used Cars, and Superstars

Patterns and Practices in Markets and Prices

Let's return to that weekend yard sale where you traded your old TV to your neighbor for a set of four books. As you will recall, we used this as an example of what might be the purest of market transactions. We assumed that the trade you made was quickly and simply done, but now let's make it a little more complicated. Let's say your neighbor only offers you two of the books for your TV and you tell her you won't make the trade for anything other than the whole collection. In other words, you start to haggle over the price.

What is haggling about? There is actually quite a bit going on here. By looking at bargaining over a price we can start to get a sense of how markets can differ in interesting ways. The first point is that markets are not purely and simply about trading goods and money. They are, after all, interactions between people, and people get a lot out of their relations with others. For some people bargaining can be an important form of social interaction and entertainment quite independent of the good and the price. If that's the case, then the final outcome about the price may be less important than the process of the bargaining itself. As we found earlier, both sides gain from voluntary trade. If the process of haggling is valued in itself, it can add to the gains that both sides make from the trade and may help to overcome any hesitation the participants have in coming to a deal.

It could well be the case, of course, that the focus in haggling is solely on the price. In that case, then the bargaining is about who is going to gain the most from the trade. If your neighbor really wants your old TV and would gain by giving you the entire set of four books for it, then she would get a better deal if she only has to give you two of the books. She can then sell the other two books and buy something else. If you sense she really wants the TV, you can capture some of that extra value from her by holding out for the entire collection of four books. Haggling, then, is a way to divide up the gains from trade between the buyer and the seller. If the original price does not allow both people to gain from the trade, changing the price can sometimes make the trade attractive to both and allow an exchange to take place that would not occur otherwise.

If the right data are available, it turns out that you can actually estimate the division of gains that go to buyers and sellers in haggling over prices in voluntary transactions. Meghan Busse, Jorge Silva-Risso, and Florian Zettel-meyer reported in an article that they had access to data that allowed them to compare how automobile manufacturer rebates in California in the late 1990s were divided between car dealers and car buyers. Since car sales are voluntary agreements, there would have been mutual gains from the deals without the rebates. Busse, Silva-Risso, and Zettelmeyer could not calculate these gains. The manufacturer rebates, however, were an added dollar amount for the buyer and seller to bargain over, and Busse, Silva-Risso, and Zettelmeyer were able to estimate how these gains were divided.

During the time period covered by the data, auto manufacturers gave both dealer rebates and customer rebates. Car buyers knew about the customer rebates because they were widely advertised. Unless they were particularly knowledgeable buyers, however, customers generally did not know about the dealer rebates. Given this difference in knowledge, you might expect that car buyers would get a good share of the consumer rebates, but, since few buyers knew about the dealer rebates, you might expect that car dealers would keep most of the dealer rebates. Busse, Silva-Risso, and Zettelmeyer found exactly this pattern. In their data set, haggling between buyers and sellers led to final prices where car buyers got from 70 percent to 90 percent of the customer rebates but only from 30 percent to 40 percent of the dealer rebates.

We actually don't do much haggling over prices in the United States. Instead, we pay fixed prices for most everyday goods. We don't haggle over the price of a loaf of bread at the grocery store, negotiate for a better deal on a tall latte at the corner coffee shop, or bargain over the price of a large pep-peroni pizza from our favorite restaurant. We do, however, haggle over the price of a new car, the tuition discount at a university, and what we pay for a new house. Why the difference?

Clearly an important factor in the United States is the price of the good relative to our income. Cars, college educations, and houses are very expensive goods. Because we tend to be pretty well off in the United States, in order to save the time of constantly haggling over price, we have become used to paying marked prices for most low-priced, everyday goods. When things get expensive, however, like for cars, college educations, and houses, then taking the time to negotiate becomes worth it. Haggling for a 10 percent discount on a $300,000 house or a $30,000 car is clearly a more valuable use of time than getting 10 percent off on a $30 can of paint.

If you think about haggling in this way, some other implications come to mind. One is that prices are inherently negotiable. It may feel uncomfortable at first, but if you give it a try you may well be able to haggle a lower price on that coffee table you are interested in at the antique store down the block or even on your next purchase of a refrigerator for your kitchen. A former student who worked in sales for a national electronics chain store told me that basically every price in the store was negotiable. *Consumer Reports*, a consumer magazine that provides advice on product quality and prices, advises its readers to bargain on all big-ticket household items. In a survey of 2,000 American adults about their haggling habits, *Consumer Reports* found that about half of those surveyed had haggled over prices during the past three years with a success rate of around 90 percent for appliances, jewelry, furniture, antiques, and personal electronics. Some stores even give employees at different levels— from floor clerks to section managers—explicit percentages that they are allowed to give customers who ask for discounts. The last time my wife and I tried it, the sales clerk passed us on to the store manager who gave us 20 percent off the clearance price in a furniture store for a nice entry table for our house. The results were encouraging enough for us to give it a try again.

Another implication is that if you go to a place where people are not as well off as in the United States, then the range of prices people are willing to take the time to negotiate will probably be greater. If you have traveled much around the world, you probably have come across situations where prices are negotiated for many everyday goods. A third implication is that the price is not the only cost you incur when you buy a good. One reason we pay marked prices without haggling in the United States is to avoid the time involved in negotiating an agreed outcome. This suggests that if the time it takes to haggle over price falls in the United States, people will do more of it. When my daughter shops, she checks for coupons and competitors' prices on her smartphone. Since this takes little time to do, she haggles over prices more often than I do. A 2013 study by the Boston Consulting Group found that 46 percent of Americans born, like my daughter, after 1980, used their smartphones to check prices when they shopped.

Haggling over prices, then, allows trades to take place as buyers and sellers in markets search for prices that allow both sides to gain in a voluntary trade. All of this is about what happens in an individual market. What happens when we consider an economy based on thousands of these individual markets? What else do prices do, other than make exchanges easier? The answer seems quite clear. When you move from a focus on individual markets to a system of markets and prices together, a central role of prices is to tell businesses what to produce, workers where to sell their labor, and consumers what to buy with their incomes. When prices are free to change and people are free to respond to those changes, prices are the main signals that guide economic decisions.

Living in the United States, this all seems obvious and straightforward. But it doesn't have to be this way. In the economic systems that existed before the 1990s in the Soviet Union, Eastern Europe, and China, prices only played the role of guides to economic decisions to a limited degree. Markets for food and clothing and other consumer goods worked partly in this way, but labor markets and producer markets did not. People were often assigned jobs and businesses were told what goods to produce, how to produce them, and what prices to charge. Prices existed, but their common function was often as bookkeeping entries and not for the purpose of giving people signals about where to work and what to produce. Prices also were often not free to change. The price of bread in the Soviet Union was fixed for fifty years.

So, prices guide economic decisions in economic systems based on markets and prices, and allow mutually beneficial trades to take place in individual markets. If you were born and raised in a market system, you know all of this very well. The prices you have faced, after all, were a major factor in determining the job you do, the place you live, and the clothes you wear.

As you live in this world of markets and prices, you know that prices cannot only change over time but can also vary at a point in time in seemingly puzzling ways. The price of a container of your favorite soft drink may be $1.50 in your office vending machine but only $.50 at your grocery store. The value of the new car you recently bought took a big dip the minute you drove it off the lot. The superstar player on your favorite major league baseball team makes a salary that is twenty times those of his journeyman teammates. What causes these patterns? Are variations like this random, or is there some sense behind them?

As an introduction to everyday patterns in prices and markets, a good place to start is to go back again to the sale of your TV at the yard sale. First, let's consider more closely the implications of saving time by not haggling over price. Second, let's look at the fact that you, as the seller, probably know more about the condition of your TV than your neighbor, the potential buyer. Finally, let's examine some of the outcomes that can happen if you were selling a skill or talent rather than a TV. Along the way, we will find out why there are the price differences in that can of soda, why your car lost value when you drove it off the lot, and why that superstar on your favorite team earns all that money.

Candy Bars

Imagine a college student in her dorm room in the middle of the afternoon who wants to buy a candy bar. She knows that the price she will have to pay for that desirable chunk of chocolate will vary dramatically depending on where she buys it. She can get the same bar for $1.50 at the vending machine in the downstairs lounge, $1.00 at the college bookstore across campus, or $.50 at the food warehouse chain over by the freeway. Now, this may seem strange. Her favorite candy bar is exactly the same in every location. Shouldn't the same candy bar have the same price everywhere?

What explains the candy bar that ranges in price from $1.50 to $.50, or the similar situation of a 12-ounce can of soda? What it all comes down to is that the candy bar in the dorm lounge vending machine is not exactly the same product as the candy bar in the membership food warehouse across town. There are a couple of ways that the bars differ. One, of course, is that the vending machine and bookstore bars are sold as single items, but those great warehouse prices are available only if you buy in multiples. Clearly, it requires less labor for the seller to put out a box of a hundred candy bars in a food warehouse than to fill a vending machine, and this gets reflected in the price of the individual item.

More important, however, is a factor pointed out by the Greek philosopher Theophrastus over two thousand years ago, by Benjamin Franklin over two hundred years ago, and more recently by Nobel-prize-winning economists George Stigler and Gary Becker, which is the economic value of time for the buyer. When that college student is considering leaving her room to buy a candy bar, there are two components to her cost: the price of the bar and the time it takes her to get the bar. Say it takes her 5 minutes to get a bar from the vending machine, 30 minutes to walk to the bookstore and back, and 2 hours to travel to the food warehouse. The comparative prices of the candy bar in these three locations, then, are not the $1.50, $1.00, and $.50 stated originally, but $1.50 plus 5 minutes, $1.00 plus 30 minutes, and $.50 plus 120 minutes. Which bar is cheapest will depend on how the student values her time. If she is studying for a critical exam later that afternoon, the bar in the vending machine may well be by far the cheapest. If nothing is pressing and her time at the moment is quite "free," then she may choose to go to the warehouse for her chocolate fix.

The vending machine operator, then, is selling more than a candy bar. He is selling the candy bar plus convenience. The idea that many goods are really themselves plus something else is an idea that has many applications. The idea that time is often that "plus" item helps explain many common behaviors. In the United States it is simply "not worth it" to bargain over the purchase price of an ear of corn and a can of tomato soup at the corner market although it might make sense for a customer at a sidewalk store in India. It also explains why it is not likely that a busy attorney earning $500 per hour will choose to travel between Los Angeles and San Francisco by train rather than by plane. A retired couple with identical wealth as the attorney, however, may well choose the train. The fact that time has value also explains why you stop at a corner convenience store for that seriously caffeinated soft drink to keep you awake on your drive home when you may well be able to buy it cheaper at the large supermarket right across the street. The "convenience" that the corner store provides is a savings in time, and time has value. As we found when we considered haggling over garage sale items, the price is not the only thing you pay when you buy a good.

Expanding this thought a little further, we can see that what seem like identical products will not always be so. There are often "added features" of seemingly standardized products that make each of them quite different. As the example of candy bars shows, the time it takes to buy a good is often an important part of its "real" price.

There are a wide variety of other "plus" factors that can be relevant in everyday markets. In gift buying, for example, the sentiment attached to a gift is often a central part of its value. Markets for online services provide another kind of example. You can often sign up for online products like Facebook or Twitter for free, but you are in fact paying a price in the form of the personal information you share. In the years to come it would not be a surprise if antitrust laws come to define the prices charged in these markets as the subscription price plus the information provided and cases are brought based on concerns that these "product-plus" prices may be deceptive or too high.

Used Cars

Now let's consider another feature of that yard sale of your old TV. If you think about it for a minute, it's pretty obvious that one factor that can influence haggling over the price of the TV is that you know more about the condition of the set than the buyer does. Your neighbor can turn the set on and watch the picture for a while, but she can't know if that scratch mark on the cabinet is purely cosmetic or due to the set being bumped and falling off its shelf, which can affect its long-run performance.

An everyday market where this asymmetry of information can lead to dramatic effects is the market for used cars. Let's say that my treasured 1972 Toyota Carina is finally beyond repair and I have to face the reality of buying a replacement car. Money is not really a problem: I can afford a new car. But I might prefer to save some money and buy a used one if I can be sure it is of good quality. I don't have a favorite buddy I can make a deal with who trades in his new car every two years and pays attention to the care of his car like it was a centenarian millionaire uncle with no other relatives. So I decide to buy a new car. Now, anyone who has purchased a new car in the United States is aware that the minute you drive the car off the lot it becomes a used car and the price drops immediately. According to Greg Lewis, the average 2017 car lost 11 percent of its value as soon as it was driven off the lot (and 25 percent in the first year). That doesn't seem sensible; after all, the car is only 1 minute old. Why should the price of a used car be so different from that of a new car?

One explanation that can be eliminated is that the price difference is just a random outcome of market behavior. Cars are expensive items, costly to repair, and dangerous if unsafe, so buyers give careful attention to the price they pay, and they are willing to take the time to negotiate. Since there are thousands of these closely considered car sales each day, the difference between new and used car prices is not an aberration and must reflect something real. What is it?

The answer, of course, is that you have to worry more about the quality of used cars than you do about new cars. You know that if you buy a new car from a dealership, there is a chance you will get a bad car. But you sense there is a larger chance you will get a bad car if you buy a seemingly new car on the used car market. After all, why would someone who recently bought a new car want to sell it?

The problem is that as a buyer of a car you have little specific knowledge about the quality of a car you propose to buy. The seller of a used car, however, knows quite well whether the car is a good or bad one. There is a gap in knowledge here, with the seller knowing something important about the product for sale that the buyer does not. But since buyers cannot easily tell good cars from bad ones, both good and bad used cars of the same kind will tend to sell at the same price.

The increased chance in general of getting a bad used car compared to a bad new car will make buyers reluctant to pay as much for used cars as new cars, even if in some cases the used car is truly as good as the new. The lower price offered for used cars will in turn discourage the owners of good used cars from selling their cars in the used car market, because they cannot get back what they paid for their car. As a result even fewer good cars will be offered in the used car market.

According to George Akerlof, who entitled his article on this problem "The Market for 'Lemons,'" a kind of Gresham's law is at work in the used car market. Gresham's law—the maxim that "bad money drives out the good"—was originally a commentary on the fact that equal-face-value clipped or shaved coins quickly replace good quality coins in the marketplace because the good quality coins could be melted down to buy more goods than the poor quality coins. Akerlof pointed out, however, that the analogy was not perfect; both buyers and sellers can tell the difference between good and bad money but not between good and bad cars. It is the fact that both good and bad used cars sell at the same price because of an asymmetry in information that causes the bad cars to drive the good cars from the market. The ultimate consequence of all this is that used cars will sell at a high discount compared to new cars.

One interesting implication of this argument is that the new/used car price gap will be different for cars of different durability and quality. If a car has a poor reputation for quality, the new/used car price gap should be significant. As a car acquires a better reputation for durability and quality, the price gap should narrow. In recent years in the United States, as the quality of many cars has improved due to competitive pressures, their new/used car price gaps have indeed decreased.

The used car market illustrates a common way that markets can vary from ideal conditions. Ideally, all buyers and all sellers would know equally all the information relevant to the good in question. This assumption breaks down if important information about the product is known only to people on one side of the market. This actually happens quite often in the markets we deal with every day as consumers. We already saw an example in the article by Busse, Silva-Risso, and Zettelmeyer on the division of dealer and consumer rebates between new car dealers and buyers. As you will recall, in their sample buyers got from 70 percent to 90 percent of the customer rebates but only from 30 percent to 40 percent of the dealer rebates. The reason for the difference was that the dealers knew about both kinds of rebates, but not all buyers knew about the rebates available to dealers.

This difference in knowledge is almost certainly true as well for the sale of your TV at the garage sale. You know more about the condition and history of your old TV than the buyer. As a result, you would expect the same pattern of price differences between new and used TVs as for new and used cars, but since it is easier for the buyer to judge the quality of a used TV by simply hooking it up and changing the channels you would expect the gap in information between buyer and seller to be less severe than it is with respect to new and used cars.

Superstars

You can only sell your TV to one person. What would happen if you could sell it to many people at once? That is a ridiculous question to ask about a TV, but in fact some lucky people have the good fortune to be able to do this with another type of good that they own: their talents. It turns out that this is a key factor in explaining superstar incomes.

Anyone who pays attention to salaries in the United States knows that the people at the top of some professions get paid astronomical salaries. We would expect the superstars of professional athletics and entertainment to earn more than those with lesser ability. But should they earn so much more? Is the person on the top rung really ten times as valuable as the people just below them occupying rungs numbered four through seven? Maybe there could be an aberration in one or two markets because of particular circumstances, but the pattern appears again and again. Why?

The money paid for the skills and talents of superstar athletes and entertainers seems outrageous. Three players in Major League Baseball earned over $20 million per year in 2008: forty-one earned that much in 2018. How high will salaries go? The fact that people at the top of their profession make more than those below them is not a surprise; every left-handed pitcher is not the same in baseball, and one hard-rock band is not like every other hard-rock band. People have different talents and levels of ability, and as a result you would expect a difference in the level of their pay. We also know that the incomes people earn make a great deal of difference in an economy like the United States, so it is not a surprise that salaries are a price that people are willing to spend a good deal of time negotiating. The negotiating is exactly the same process as haggling over the price of your old TV at the yard sale. Yet the top players on professional baseball teams can end up making twenty times the pay of those at the bottom. It seems there must be something else going on here.

Sherwin Rosen looked at this issue in an article entitled "The Economics of Superstars." According to Rosen, two factors come together to create the huge salaries of superstars. The first factor is consumer tastes. One of Rosen's examples was the best surgeon in town; if that surgeon is 10 percent more effective in saving lives than anyone else, people will be willing to pay more than 10 percent extra to be her patient. The same holds true for quarterbacks in football or opera stars; the demand to see the very best perform in some fields expands more than the differential in skill.

This first factor guarantees that stars in professions with this feature will gain a disproportionate amount of the income earned in their field. Another factor is necessary, however, to explain why incomes are as high as they are today. In these markets, the time and energy required from a performer is about the same whether they have an audience of 10 or an audience of 10,000. It takes about the same effort to produce a novel or pitch a baseball game, for example, no matter how large the audience. But in markets with extraordinary superstar incomes, the performer is able to charge a fee to everyone who uses their services. Thus the author who sells 1,000,000 copies of every novel will do much better than the one who sells 10,000. In markets for talent that have the features of being able to sell to more than one person at a time and being able to charge a fee to each buyer, the incomes of superstars will not just be disproportionately higher than those of near competitors; they may be stratospheric. To see how well finding ways to link a large audience to pay can work, just recall the case of the family that earned $22 million in 2018 from toy producers by making YouTube videos of their seven-year-old son playing with the producers' toys.

Two differences from the sale of your TV at the yard sale come together, then, to generate the levels of superstar income we see in some fields. First, the talents of individual performers are seen by consumers as very different; a performance by the best opera tenor in the world can be worth more to fans than a production with numbers three and four together. Second, unlike a yard sale where the product is sold to one buyer at a time, in superstar markets one seller can sell his services to a large number of buyers at the same time. The first difference causes incomes in the field to be biased in favor of the top performers; the second is needed to generate extraordinary levels of income. Unfortunately for the top surgeon in Rosen's example, only the first factor will be at work in determining her income. She can expect to earn significantly more than other surgeons in town, but because she cannot yet perform surgery on large numbers of patients at once, she is unlikely to earn rock-star or home-run-king levels of income.

CHAPTER TWO

401(k)s, Lotto, Cell Phone Plans, and Diamonds

Structural and Behavioral Factors and Market Prices

The price patterns in the markets for candy bars, superstars, and used cars seem to be very different. Candy bar prices can vary widely in even a small geographical area. New car prices drop significantly the minute the cars become used. And superstars can have incomes dramatically higher than their closest rivals. Since you have to deal with price patterns like this every day, you will be glad to know that these are not the result of a hopeless mishmash of cause and effect and that it is not too difficult to make sense out of this diversity. A close look at the factors that lie behind the price patterns in markets reveals that the reasons for their differences can be grouped into two broad categories. The first group includes behavioral factors that relate to the attitudes, biases, and tendencies that people bring with them when they are involved in market transactions. The second involves structural factors that relate to such things as the number of buyers and sellers in markets, the characteristics of the products being sold, and the conditions that limit or allow the entry of new customers or producers. Together, structural and behavioral factors combine to create what consumers experience in everyday markets.

The haggling that took place over the rebates for new cars in the Busse, Silva-Risso, and Zettelmeyer study, for example, is a behavioral factor. It is an interaction between people that can have value in itself and thus can affect the market price. The fact that people more than proportionally value talent in some professions is a behavioral factor in the superstar market. This, as you will recall, explains why the best surgeon in town will do very well in her profession even though she can sell her skills to only one person at a time. The importance of time in buying a candy bar, on the other hand, is a structural factor. It is not just the bar that matters in its price but the time it takes to find and purchase the bar. The gaps in knowledge between buyers and sellers in the new car rebate market and in the used car market are also structural. It is clear from the price patterns in car markets that when buyers and sellers bring different information to markets there can be critical consequences for their outcomes. As George Akerlof pointed out in his article on the market for used cars, if the gap in knowledge is extreme enough, then the market may break down completely and totally cease to exist.

In some markets, structural features play the primary role in explaining the patterns that exist. This is the case in the market for candy bars, where time and convenience are the key factors at work. This also is true in the market for used cars, where the information gap between buyers and sellers is the central factor. In other markets, both behavioral and structural factors play important roles. As we saw, this is the case in the market for superstars. The fact that a surgeon can sell her services to only one person at a time while a major league pitcher can perform for an audience of millions is a critical structural feature explaining the difference in their salaries, while the fact that people are willing to pay more than proportionally to experience the skills of some professions is a critical behavioral feature in creating the income gaps between the best and the near best in many occupations.

The fact that the causes of the patterns we see in everyday markets and prices can be divided into specific structural and behavioral factors is important to know. It can help make dealing with markets and prices a bit easier. It means that the patterns we see in the prices and markets around us are not random or mysterious events but understandable consequences of specific market characteristics. If you have a good idea about the behaviors and the structures that come together to create the prices you see in the markets you encounter, then you can come up with strategies to better deal with them.

The structural factors that influence prices and markets have been a central topic of introductory economics courses for decades. In beginning texts in economics the main structural factors that get attention are the number of firms in the market, the similarity of goods sold by different firms, and how easy it is for new firms to enter markets. If markets have very many sellers, goods that are identical between sellers, and low barriers to entry, then the expectation is that the market will be very competitive and prices will be close to costs of production. Producers of Red Delicious apples, for example, are in a market like this, with literally thousands of individual producers in the United States, nearly identical products, and low barriers to entry. At the other extreme, in a market with one seller, a unique product, and high barriers to entry, the expectation is that there will be very little competition in the market and prices may well be much higher than the costs of production. Having near monopolies in the goods their firms controlled created fortunes for John D. Rockefeller and Standard Oil, Edmund Land and Polaroid, and Bill Gates and Microsoft. Firms in markets that fall between these extremes will have price and profit results that are intermediate between those in monopoly and competitive markets.

As the candy bars, used cars, and superstars markets indicate, however, the list of important structural features that matter in determining the patterns we see in everyday prices and market is longer than that typically covered in introductory texts. Candy bars are an example of a "good-plus" market, in this instance with the "plus" that matters being the time it takes to buy the bar. In the used car and new car rebate markets, the structural difference that matters is an information gap between buyers and sellers. In the case of superstars, the key structural factor is the ability for individuals to sell their services to large numbers of customers at the same time.

Although structural factors have been seen as important in explaining patterns of everyday prices and markets for decades, it is only more recently that behavioral factors have received equal emphasis. The Nobel Prize in economics has been around since 1969, and prizes have been awarded to contributions related to the structural features of markets since the early 1980s, but the first prize for analysis of behavioral factors in markets was awarded to Daniel Kahneman in 2002. A main insight from studies of behavioral factors in markets is that although the biases and tendencies in human behavior that people bring with them when they deal with markets and prices can be helpful and make good sense in many realms of daily life, these biases and tendencies can create problems for people when it comes to making economic decisions. To get a sense of how these behavioral tendencies can work, let's look at patterns of outcomes in prices and markets related to retirement planning, playing the state lotto, purchasing a cell phone plan, and buying diamonds.

401(k)s

I must admit that putting things off until later is a pretty common pattern in my personal behavior. This is harmless in many cases—what does it matter, really, if I don't get around to weeding that flowerbed along the side of the house until next month? The very human tendency to procrastinate makes good sense in most dimensions of daily life. We need to be able to prioritize, to identify and take care of the important things, to do first things first and think about less urgent matters later. But putting things off can have serious consequences when it comes to making decisions about money. People can get themselves into a real economic mess by procrastination.

One of the important ways this happens to many people is in their retirement planning. You know very well that you should have started contributing to that 401(k) plan earlier, but you just didn't get around to it. In order to sign up you had to go down to the Human Resources Department and fill out a pile of forms, and it was just never convenient. In the early 2000s, as policy makers became increasingly concerned about the lack of adequate retirement planning by people and as researchers looked at what is going on here, this behavior became strikingly evident as a very normal practice. The "default choice" in most retirement plans was to not participate, and even though workers knew they should go down to Human Resources and sign up for retirement plans, they commonly put it off.

People who were concerned about this pattern convinced some firms to change their retirement programs from an "opt-in" to an "opt-out" structure. New employees were automatically enrolled in the retirement program at a basic level and had to go to Human Resources and sign the forms if they wanted not to participate. The results were often dramatic. In one case, the participation rate of newly hired employees increased from 49 percent to 86 percent. These results were so striking and so compelling that the U.S. Congress passed the Pension Reform Act of 2006 to change the rules so that the default option in 401(k) programs could be more easily switched to automatic enrollment with an opt-out provision.

The underparticipation in retirement programs actually seems to be the result of two common behaviors. One is procrastination, and the second is that we don't value things in the future as highly as we do the same things in the present. If I offer to give you $10 today or $10 a year from now, you will certainly take the $10 now. The reasons are obvious. The $10 now is a sure thing, but the $10 in the future is not at all certain for all kinds of reasons. You may not trust me to follow through with my promise or, infinitely worse, one of us might die before the year is up and you can collect. The fact that the future is uncertain biases all of our economic decisions to focus on the present. As a result, it is very hard to convince someone who is twenty years old that they should start now to save for a retirement perhaps fifty years in the future.

For the same reason that we value a dollar today more than a dollar tomorrow, if I am going to convince you to give me $250 as a loan for the next five years, I am going to have to bribe you to give up the opportunity to spend the $250 on yourself today. There is certainly some amount I can offer that will make you agree to the deal. Depending on how much you trust me and how much faith you have in the stability of the future, maybe an offer of $500 in five years will do it. That extra amount of money—that bribe—is what we call interest. In fact, human attitudes about the difference between the present and the future are the foundation for why interest even exists. If you think about it, if the present and the future are exactly the same to you, then you wouldn't need that bribe to put off spending your money and you would be equally willing to take that $10 offered to you either today or a year from now.

In order to help people overcome their biases toward inadequate saving for the future, some companies have created retirement plans that not only have an opt-out feature but also include automatically increasing levels of contributions as pay increases. The Save More Tomorrow program developed by Richard Thaler and Shlomo Benartzi, for example, has people participate at a minimal level and then slowly increase their level of contributions over time. In a recent book Thaler describes dramatic increases in participation rates in both basic retirement and in Save More Tomorrow programs from using an opt-out feature.

Our hardwired attitudes toward the future and about procrastination obviously can affect our economic well-being. The incomes we earn have to take care of us both today and in distant tomorrows. How well off we are today is constrained by the prices we face in markets, and how well off we are tomorrow is constrained by our attitudes about procrastination and about the future. The obvious strategy to deal with the economic issues created by procrastinating and discounting the future is to be aware of this tendency, set a firm date to set up that retirement program, and follow through in your long-term planning. You know you should contribute more to that 401(k) and start that IRA, and now that you know why you haven't done it, hopefully you will.

Lotto

One way to break the constraints created by the prices we face compared to our incomes is, of course, to win the lottery. I buy a ticket now and then—those billion dollar jackpots just seem worth giving it a try. But in general I don't. The lottery just doesn't seem fair.

It turns out that attitudes toward fairness can affect markets and prices in a way similar to our attitudes toward the future. Both attitudes about the future and about fairness are very human reactions that influence how we make decisions about what we do with our incomes. One way that attitudes toward fairness come into play in markets can be demonstrated by an experiment called the ultimatum game. In this game, two people are brought into a room. One of the players is given an amount of money, say $100, and told that they have to make a one-time offer to split the money with the other player. The player with the $100 can offer anything they want, from zero to the whole thing. The only rule in the game is that if the second player accepts the offer, then the split is made, and both people walk away with what they agreed on. If, however, the second player refuses the offer, then both players receive nothing.

You might think that the second player would always accept any positive offer, even if only 1 cent out of a $100. After all, both players start the game with nothing and end it with money in hand, and even something small is better than nothing. In fact, this is not what happens. The result of hundreds of repetitions with people all over the world is that offers that are much less than a 70/30 split are often rejected. I have done this experiment in classes (using $1 instead of $100—no superstar income for me to toss around here), and in every case some of the offers to split the money have been turned down. People have an innate sense of fairness, it seems, that affects how they react to prices and markets.

Feelings about fairness also affect our attitudes about taking a chance. Say you are offered a gamble on flipping a coin. The coin is honest, in that the chance of getting heads or tails is the same. The gamble is that you earn $X if the coin turns up heads and lose $100 if it turns up tails. How much does $X need to be for you to be willing to play the game? The result of offering this chance to multitudes of people is that the usual response is somewhere around $200. People in general want to be assured of a payoff that is about twice the possible loss in order to take the risk.

This means that it takes a potential gain that is more than the potential loss to make taking a risk seem fair to many people. The pain of a $100 loss is more than the gain from a $100 win. The fact that a loss seems more painful than an equal gain has been used to explain the outcomes of the coffee mug experiments referred to earlier, the performance of professional golfers, and, surprisingly, as part of an evolutionary biology explanation for why people believe in God. After the mugs are distributed in the coffee mugs experiments and people are asked what they would be willing to sell and buy them for, the price put on the mugs by their owners is more than what the others are willing to pay. The pain from the loss of giving up the mug seems to people to be more than the value of getting one. In the case of professional golfers, Devin Pope and Maurice Schweitzer compared the success of identical putts for a birdie and for a par using a data set containing details of two and a half million putts on the Professional Golfers' Association tour. Taking everything they could think of into account, Pope and Schweitzer found that professional golfers are 2 to 4 percent more likely to make comparable par putts than birdie putts. The pain of going one stroke over par, in other words, is more than the gain of scoring one stroke under par, and this shows up in performance. In his book *God Is Watching You*, Dominic Johnson argues that the tendency to put more emphasis on a loss than a gain is one factor behind belief in a watchful, vengeful God. According to Johnson, this belief helps people avoid bad acts that harm themselves or those around them.

It should be no surprise that people's attitudes about fairness and losses can affect the outcomes of markets and prices. These attitudes probably do not create too many problems, however, for people in dealing with everyday prices and markets. On the negative side, as the results of the ultimatum game show, these tendencies can create circumstances where people do not take gains they can easily make. Balancing things out on the positive side, however, is the fact that being wary about losses can help keep people from taking too many potentially dangerous financial risks.

Cell Phone Plans

It seems that everyone today has a cell phone. The way things are going, the day will soon come when there are more cell phones in the world than the number of people. That's kind of interesting to think about and probably brings a pensive look to your face. The day might come as well when it is hardly possible to find a place to stand anywhere in the world and not see a cell phone tower looming on the horizon. That is a less engaging thought to come to mind and may turn your pensive look into a frown.

It has actually been fun to follow the changes in cell phone use. Who knew that phones could be a fashion good? With all the styles and features to choose from today, it takes some effort to remember that the standard used to be the old basic black dial phone on the hallway stand. Of course, there were some style options even back then—it's hard to believe that the Princess model in pink was ever a hot item—so maybe the current range of options could have been expected. It is more of a surprise, perhaps, to think that you know people who have been using phones for years and have never dialed a call in their life. It is probably even the case that you know people who have never punched buttons on a phone to make a call. You may even have friends who don't even know how to use their cell phone to make a phone call. All they do is text.

This is all very interesting to think about, until you have to pay the cell phone bill. If you are the one paying the bills and you go back far enough to remember only having a phone in the hallway, you probably know that you are paying more now for phone service than you did before you made the switch. Since literally tens of millions of people have decided to buy cell phones, this is obviously a choice that has such appeal that it is worth the extra cost.

If you pay the bills, you know as well that a common plan for cell phones in the United States involves a fixed monthly fee, an allowance for minutes usage covered by the fee, and then a fairly high charge for usage beyond the allowance. You may have come across a similar pricing system if you lease your car. Charging for cell phone use doesn't have to be this way, of course. You paid for your old home phone by a monthly fee and a long-distance charge for every minute called. In looking at the cell phone market, Michael Grubb was interested in this common pricing structure for cell phone use and decided to look into what was going on.

After reviewing the possible reasons for a pricing structure of fixed fees, set allowances, and high overuse charges, Grubb narrowed the explanations to two possibilities. Firms may be using this structure as a way to charge different customers different prices for the same good based on their willingness to pay. When he checked the implications of this explanation against plan choices made by 2,332 students at a major university over a nearly four-year period, however, Grubb found that the data were more consistent with his second possible explanation for the common cell phone pricing structure.

Grubb's second explanation was based on one of the behavioral biases people carry around with them that affects their decisions when they deal with prices and markets. Grubb found that the best explanation for the common cell phone pricing structure of a fixed fee, an allowance, and high overuse charges was a bias that people have to be overconfident. It turns out that optimism seems to apply to all areas of human decisions. As Richard Thaler and Cass Sunstein report in an overview of biases in economic behavior, people routinely overestimate their chance of success in starting a small business, having a successful marriage, and winning the lottery. By far the majority of students, teachers, and drivers report in opinion surveys that they think they are above average. Given the pervasiveness of this bias, it shouldn't be a surprise that firms will take advantage of it in their pricing if they can.

The overconfidence that comes into play in using cell phones, according to Grubb, is people's estimates of the amount they will use the phone. People, in fact, have a poor sense of their actual usage and tend to overestimate or underestimate what they do. If they overestimate, they pay a higher average price per minute used than they expected because of the fixed fee. If they underestimate, they pay the high overuse fees. Given the tendencies of consumers to be overconfident about their actual use, Grubb finds that the common pricing structure we see for cell phones is the optimal one from the phone companies' point of view.

Of course, some people will learn over time and change their plan to fit their actual use. If everyone did this regularly, the best pricing structure for cell phones may well be different. If you pay attention to the ads you see about cell phone services, you know that alternatives do exist and that the pricing structures in the industry are evolving. But the phone companies can rely on another inherent tendency that people have that affects their personal and economic decisions, and that is a bias not to change. As Thaler and Sunstein report, this status quo bias is behind a lot of poor economic decisions. Although investment advisers always tell people to check the allocation of their retirement accounts over time, few people do. The bias to stay with the current situation is why magazine and computer app producers love to sign you up for automatic renewal of subscriptions. Given a situation where people are commonly far wrong about how much they actually use their cell phones and where they have a bias not to change their plans, you get a pricing structure like the one you see when you pay your cell phone bill each month.

What it all comes down to in the end is that you really should check your usage and see if you can do better by changing your current plan. The combination of a bias to be overconfident and a bias to stay with the status quo creates the possibility for overpaying for that cell phone service that has become a near necessity in the lives of many people.

Diamonds

Diamonds really are special. They have both industrial uses as unglamorous machine parts in grinding and drilling and consumer uses as spectacular and beautiful jewelry. The market that links the mines where diamonds are found to the firms who make industrial equipment and consumer adornments is not competitive at all. There are very few sources of diamonds in the world, and these sources are owned by even fewer firms. Once diamonds get into the hands of jewelry makers, however, things change. The cutting and polishing and marketing of final gems is a very competitive business.

Frank Scott and Aaron Yelowitz became interested in the consumer part of the diamond business because it has become even more competitive in recent years with the development of online markets. When you wanted to buy an engagement ring in the past, you drove around to visit the jewelry stores in your area to see what was available. Today, you can shop the world. You can now find extensive information on shape, color, size, and price to guide your decision. Scott and Yelowitz found the online guides to be clear and informative and a great consumer resource. To see how things are working out in this new world of stronger competition, Scott and Yelowitz collected price data on over 135,000 diamonds sold on three major online sites.

The authors found something interesting. Taking quality into account, they found that diamond prices, as you would expect, rise as carat size (diamond weight) increases. What they also found, however, was that there were clear breaks in prices at specific carat sizes. These "focal points," as Scott and Yelowitz called them, came at 0.5, 1.0, 1.5, and 2.0 carats. In their sample, the difference in price from a 0.99 carat diamond to a 1.00 carat diamond was $554, while the difference between a 1.00 and 1.01 carat diamond was $120. The difference in price between a 0.49 and a 0.50 carat diamond was $281, while the difference between a 0.50 and 0.51 carat diamond was only $23.

It was very clear in their sample that diamonds at or above a certain size have a premium price. This is a very competitive market on both the supply and the demand side with hundreds of buyers and sellers and plenty of good information available to everyone, so why the price breaks? Scott and Yelowitz looked at several possible explanations and decided in the end that it all come down to the behavioral fact that consumers really do see diamonds as special. They found that the major part of the market for larger gem-quality diamonds is engagement rings. Now it is certainly possible to purchase a 0.98 carat diamond and say it is a 1.00 carat stone. This might even be fairly common when people buy jewelry that they wear themselves. But who is going to do this with an engagement ring? There is something quite different in the interpersonal relations and status of buying and giving an engagement ring from other uses of diamonds. As Scott and Yelowitz found, the special significance of diamonds in engagement rings shows up clearly in the prices that people pay for the diamonds they buy.

The existence of "focal points" shows up in patterns of other prices as well. In baseball, a batting average of .300 or above is viewed as a sign of excellence. A .299 hitter is not viewed in the same way. As a result, it should not be a surprise that no .299 hitter took a walk (which has no effect on the batting average) in the last game of the season for thirty-five years. Every one of them tried for that last hit every time they came up to bat that would carry them to excellence. It should also not be a surprise to learn that the 0.3 percent increase in a batting average from .299 to .300 carried with it an average 2.0 percent increase in salary over that same time period. There is a jump in salaries, in other words, at the .300 mark that is equivalent to the jump in prices at the 1.00 carat size in diamonds.

The fact that focal points exist in some markets creates the opportunity to do a bit better for yourself when you encounter them. If you want to buy an item with a diamond in its design, it is an excellent idea to check on the prices using a 0.98 and a 1.02 carat stone. Overall, the message from retirement planning, taking a risk, selecting a cell phone plan, and buying a diamond seems clear. The behavioral biases and attitudes people carry with them can have significant effects on the patterns we see in everyday markets and prices, and by knowing these patterns you can act to do better for yourself in dealing with them.

CHAPTER THREE

Fashion, Fads, and Brands

Information Gaps as a Structural Factor

We've made a good start in looking for reasons for the prices and pricing patterns we see in everyday markets. It is encouraging to know that understandable structural and behavioral factors lie behind these patterns, including, as we have seen so far, structural factors like different information being known by buyers and sellers and the fact that some goods can be sold to more than one person at the same time, and behavioral factors like the tendencies to procrastinate, to be overconfident, and to be reluctant to change the status quo. It is the particular mix of these structural and behavioral features that creates the interesting markets that are the focus of these chapters. As we have seen, these features play out in different ways in different markets depending on the combination of structural and behavioral factors at work.

The previous chapter looked at markets heavily influenced by behavioral factors. Let's return in this chapter to the structural side. It turns out that different kinds of gaps in information between buyers and sellers are important in explaining the patterns we see in many markets. In the used car market, for example, issues are created by buyers not knowing everything that sellers know about the quality of used cars. But what would happen if the situation is reversed? What if the seller of a product doesn't know something that the buyer knows? A first reaction might be to ask how that could even matter. After all, a buyer is just a buyer, aren't they? In fact, the answer in some markets is clearly no. It turns out that the reasons some goods are "fashion" goods has a lot to do with information that buyers have that sellers do not know.

It doesn't take much experience in a market economy to discover that information gaps of one kind or another are a common feature in consumer goods markets. At the very least, the details of differences in products sold by firms in the same market create the possibility for information problems. How, as a consumer, can you know if the differences between Golden Crunchy Corn Flakes and Toasted Munchy Corn Flakes really matter? This lack of perfect information creates several kinds of effects. An important one is that an opportunity is created for firms to provide objective information about goods. That is what publications like *Consumer Reports* and websites like Angie's List or Yelp are all about. Do you want to know about the qualities of different kinds of house paint, spaghetti sauce, air conditioners, or T-shirts? Check out the reviews in publications like *Consumer Reports*. Do you want to know the quality of work done by local plumbers, roofers, electricians, or insulation contractors? Check out the reviews on websites like Angie's List or Yelp. Used with a sensible degree of caution about the objective quality of the reviews, consulting sources like these can be a very useful consumer strategy. I use these sources regularly for one reason or another, and the fact that I keep going back to them is evidence enough that I have often found them to be helpful guides in making consumption decisions.

Another effect of product differentiation and imperfect information in common consumer markets is that the opportunity is created for the existence of fashion, fads, and brands. The very existence of fashion, fads, and brands— market realities whose existence makes the heart beat faster in all serious shoppers—is due in one way or another to the details of gaps in information between buyers and sellers. Fashion goods are those where style is an important part of the product. You do not just buy a blouse, but a summer blouse in lemon yellow with a scalloped neckline made of 100 percent pima cotton. Fads exist when suddenly everyone just has to have a hula hoop, pet rock, Cabbage Patch doll, or Razor scooter. Brands are names attached to goods. When you have a cold and want a box of facial tissues, you may well ask for a Kleenex. It turns out that the existence of information gaps between buyers and sellers is an important factor behind all of these practices. What is going on here?

Fashion

What exactly does it mean to say that a product is one where fashion is important? If we look at goods like women's clothes or new cars, which almost everyone agrees are fashion-oriented, several features seem to stand out. One, certainly, is that there are frequent style changes. Another is the "obsolescence" of older products. What fashionista, after all, really wants to be seen wearing a coat with last year's lapel width or in last season's shade of green? In the market for sports shoes, about three-fourths of new trainers are for sale for less than a year. These characteristics are obvious to anyone who pays even the slightest attention to fashionable goods. Another feature is equally obvious to those who more closely follow fashion goods—the decline in the price of fashion goods over the product season. The common pattern here is that when new goods are introduced, sellers give them a high price. Then, as the season progresses, prices tend to fall. At the beginning of a new season, the price cycle starts again.

Why does this regular price cycle exist? Peter Pashigian and Brian Bowen in an article on the topic considered several explanations for the seasonal price cycle in fashion goods and concluded that the explanation that best fits the evidence is lack of perfect information about buyers' tastes in the marketplace. An information gap exists, in other words, but one that is just the reverse of the one in the used car market. The argument here, using women's dresses as an example, is that at the start of the season, sellers do not know which of their bright and stylish products will be best sellers. As a result, they charge high prices for all new dresses. As the season progresses, some colors, fabrics, and trim designs will sell well, some so-so, and others not at all. Sellers respond by lowering prices over time. By the end of the season, store racks are full of seasonal clearance dresses, at substantial markdowns, which are dominated by the colors, fabrics, and designs few people wanted. If sellers had perfect knowledge about buyers' tastes, they would not have been stuck with this dross. Thus seller uncertainty about consumer tastes for products that are dominated by style generates seasonal price cycles.

If this argument is right, one would expect that products that are more "fashionable"—that is, characterized by more frequent and substantial changes in style—should have greater seasonal price swings. This is exactly what Pashigian and Bowen found. They found greater seasonal cycles for women's outer garments than women's under garments, for more expensive men's dress shirts than less expensive lines, and for teenage and young-adult clothes than for adult clothing. These variations seem to accord well with goods that are usually seen as more dominated by "fashion." Changes over the years in the size of seasonal price swings also fit the argument nicely. White was the most popular color by far for men's dress shirts and bed sheets up to the mid-1960s. Since then, colors and patterns of all kinds have become the norm. Consistent with the imperfect-information explanation of seasonal price changes for fashion goods, one significant consequence of the greater variety in men's dress shirts and bed sheets has been a more pronounced seasonal swing in their prices.

Building on the idea that uncertainty causes price cycles in fashion goods, a later article by Pashigian and Bowen in conjunction with Eric Gould puzzled over the fact that seasonal price cycles became more extreme between the mid-1950s and the late 1980s in women's apparel but less extreme for new cars. The seasonal cycle continued to exist for new cars, but while in the mid-1950s newly introduced cars sold in November for about 5 percent above the annual average and in September for 4 percent below the annual average, by the late

1980s the annual price change had been reduced so that new cars sold at prices only about 1 percent above the annual average in November and 1 percent below the annual average in September. Over the same period that price cycles were becoming less pronounced in new cars, they rose significantly for women's apparel. Where early-season prices were about 1 percent above the annual average and end-of-season prices 1 percent below the annual average in the mid-1950s, by the late 1980s early-season prices were over 5 percent above the annual average and late-season prices over 3 percent below the annual average.

What caused the decline in the seasonal price cycle for cars over this time period while it increased for women's clothing? Was it just a whim of consumer tastes, so that people no longer responded to style changes in cars like they once did? After examining the industries in detail, Pashigian, Bowen, and Gould decided that in fact what happened was that cars became less of a fashion good between the mid-1950s and the late 1980s while women's clothing became more fashion-oriented. The importance of annual style changes moved in opposite directions in the two industries.

And what caused this? Was the change in the significance of style simply due to producer responses to consumer buying habits? To a degree this may have been so, but Pashigian, Bowen, and Gould found perhaps a more fundamental factor at work. Over time, the technology of producing women's clothing and new cars changed in such a way that it became cheaper to produce significant style changes in women's clothing and more expensive to do so in new cars. Because the costs of production changed in such a way that cars became characterized by more infrequent style changes than in the past, cars became less of a fashion good than they were. New kinds of weaving and knitting machinery caused just the opposite effect in women's clothing.

This conclusion has a couple of interesting implications. One is that not all consumer goods can be fashion goods; production techniques have to allow frequent style changes. In the sports shoes market, firms are experimenting with production techniques that reduce the time from first sketch of a new design to final product from several months to a few weeks or even days. A second interesting consequence of the change in the fashion characteristics of new cars is that another factor can be added to our evaluation of new-versus-used car prices presented earlier. In that discussion, it was mentioned that if cars acquire a reputation as being more durable and of better quality, then the new/used car price differential should fall over time. Given Pashigian, Bowen, and Gould's discussion of the decreasing "fashionability" of new cars, if cars were produced in the late 1980s with less frequent style changes, then used cars should have become "obsolete" less quickly in terms of style. This also should have worked to reduce new/used car price differentials. In fact, new/used car price differences did fall over the years, from price declines of one-year-old cars compared to new cars in the low 20 percent range in the mid-1950s to price declines in the midteen percent range in the late 1980s. Both improvements in quality and declines in style changes were at work here. A third implication is that if automobile production techniques change so that more frequent style changes are possible than in the late 1980s, then the seasonal price cycle and the new/used car price differentials should broaden again. Many production innovations for cars in the past few years seem to have moved in this direction, so it is reasonable to assume that a comparison of 1980s and 2010s car prices may show this pattern.

The message for a dedicated consumer of fashion goods is clear. Because of the fashion good price cycle, if you want to own the first and freshest new styles, then you are going to pay a premium. If you don't care much about being among the first to be seen wearing or driving the newest styles or models, you can do very well for yourself by waiting until the end of the seasonal cycle. When a colleague of mine needed a new car, for example, her husband, who knew the market intimately because he purchased dozens of cars each year as part of his job, started serious negotiations for her closeout previous-year model in mid-November and bought her new car right after Thanksgiving.

Fads

Fads happen. All of a sudden, everyone wants to eat at Joe's Veggie-Fruitie Restaurant/Bar, to drive the new XJZ920–YT Turbo car, or to buy a Golly-Gee Baby-of-Mine doll for their child. Why do such herd-like behaviors happen? Several explanations have been given for why people bunch together in their actions. One is that people in general have a taste for conformity; by doing what everyone else is doing, you feel better. Another is that people realize that if everyone does the same thing, then everyone is better off; if all drivers carefully observe stop signs and traffic signals, then driving is much safer for everyone. A third is that social sanctions cause joint behavior; you act like everyone else does because of the penalties that exist if you don't.

As these explanations suggest, following the herd appears to be a deep-seated human behavior. Like the attitudes we discussed earlier about ownership, the future, and fairness, paying attention to what others do seems to be one of those hardwired tendencies that we bring with us when we deal with everyday markets and prices. In a review of this behavior and how it affects markets, Richard Thaler and Cass Sunstein describe an experiment where a person is brought into a group of strangers, and then the group members are asked to answer very simple questions. If the person who is brought in has to answer last and everyone before them answers incorrectly, it turns out that it is very common for the last person to answer the same as those who answered before even though the answer is clearly wrong. In summarizing the results from over a hundred experiments like this in seventeen countries, Thaler and

Sunstein report that people consistently gave incorrect answers in these circumstances between 20 and 40 percent of the time. In a 2017 book looking at reasons for this behavioral tendency, Hugo Mercier and Dan Sperber argue that human reasoning evolved to establish group identity and the individual's place in the group and not to increase knowledge or make better decisions.

This behavioral urge to identify with a group provides reasons why people might act the same as others once a fad has begun, but it does not explain how fads get started in the first place or why fads often come and go so quickly. What seems to matter in the beginning of fads is our by now familiar idea of imperfect information in the marketplace. As argued by David Hirshleifer and others, fads can begin if people do not have complete knowledge about products before making decisions whether to buy, and rely on actions by others as an important source of information to close this gap.

For example, let's say that a new restaurant opens in town. At the start, everyone has limited knowledge about the place. Say that José, who is known for his discriminating taste in food, buys the first meal. Mary, who saw José eat there, adds this information to her meager knowledge about the restaurant and decides to give it a try. Now Fred, who saw José and Mary eat at the new spot, decides on the basis of their attendance to go himself. Very quickly, a snowball effect can develop. Because this snowball effect can be significant, sellers of new products often try to take advantage of it. New restaurants have been known to hire people to eat at their place in order to give the appearance of instant popularity. In a notorious example in the mid-1990s, the authors of a business strategy book bought 50,000 copies of their own book at stores across the country in order to get the book on the *New York Times* best-seller list. These are examples of attempts to create information that later buyers use in their spending decisions. In the terminology developed by Hirshleifer and his colleagues, if that snowball starts to roll, an "informational cascade" is formed.

What happens in an informational cascade is that people, because of their limited personal knowledge, rely on the actions of others to guide their own decisions. Information about others' participation can dominate individuals' limited knowledge, and people start to act the same. Hirshleifer and his colleagues have used this argument to explain why teenagers at one high school smoke and those at one across town do not, why religious movements sometimes sweep across a population, why ineffective medical procedures like bloodletting and elective hysterectomies have become popular at different times, why momentum builds for political candidates, and, of course, why fads occur for consumer goods. In an application related to Internet information, Arnout van de Rijt and colleagues conducted an experiment where he picked 200 new unfunded Kickstarter projects and randomly gave half of them a donation. Twenty-four days later, 70 percent of the one hundred projects given seed money had received at least one other donation while only 39 percent of the other projects had received any donations. In another article on the topic, Ken Hendricks and Alan Sorensen apply the idea to the sales of music, books, movies, and video games.

One of the strengths of the "cascades" idea is that it also explains why fads are fragile. The reason for this is that the start of the fad can be built on very limited information about the product. The fad begins and gathers momentum because of others' actions and not because of detailed knowledge about the product. Say that a fad develops in a cascade-like way for that Golly-Gee Baby-of-Mine doll. Now assume that a new piece of information comes out about the product; say a consumer investigative report finds that the dolls are unsafe because the skin is easily broken into sharp fragments. According to the cascades argument, new information like this can quickly stop a fad completely, and in fact can readily start a cascade in the reverse direction.

A more discouraging part of the cascades argument is that it also implies that good products or good ideas can easily fail to survive through mistaken actions by the crowd. Fads, in other words, do not always favor the best goods. If two new restaurants open at the same time across the street from one another, one may well become "faddishly" popular while the other one dies, even though the second one might have the better food and service. As Hendricks and Sorensen put it in their study of music, books, and video games, "the distribution of success in these markets may be very different from what it would be in a world with more fully informed customers." This is because the choices made by the first few buyers of a new good are critical. If they choose against a good, even if they are wrong, these actions may well seal its fate.

Interestingly, economists who try to explain social conventions have followed the same type of analysis. Conventions are patterns of social or economic behavior that have staying power, such as driving on the right-hand side of the road, wearing formal suits in business, or accounting rules. Fads and conventions are thus basically the same thing, with the key difference that fads are ephemeral and conventions enduring. As explained by H. Peyton Young, conventions have the same foundation as fads in limited knowledge and paying attention to the actions of others. What may make a fad become a convention is the intrusion of other factors once the common behavior gets going. Laws may be passed requiring everyone to drive on the same side of the road, or recognition that everyone benefits from observing stop signs can make such actions self-enforcing. In such cases, the fragility of the "cascade" is overcome, and fads can become conventions. Young argues, however, that conventions are not guaranteed forever. They are strongly supported cascades, but like any cascade there is a chance that a series of actions may occur that will cause a change in the convention. Countries actually have changed the side of the road that people drive on (Sweden went from the left to the right in 1967), and generally accepted standards of business attire do change (as in the acceptance of casual dress in many professions).

As a consumer in a market economy, it is inevitable that you will be caught up at some time in a market that has become a fad. Being aware of the urge to conform by following the herd can help you feel better about the experience. If the goal for you is mainly to identify as part of a group and do what others you care about are doing, then you can just enjoy being swept away. You know the fad will fade and the good you bought will lose its value, but if being part of the group is what it is all about for you, then the price is simply part of what you pay to take part in the experience. If the fad for you is using the actions of others as a substitute for information about the good or service, however, then you should be more cautious. It may well be that you would enjoy even more the other new restaurant across the street from the one with the faddish following, or that other new author or music group than those at the top of the charts. You should also be wary that people can try to create fads, like the authors of the business book. If you end up following a fad and spending $40 to buy a dud restaurant meal, video, or book, then the cost will not be too high and is probably small enough that you can just shrug it off and resolve to do better next time. If you are tempted, however, to follow a fad to take advantage of that "new investment opportunity that everyone is talking about," then you should be particularly cautious because the expense involved may be significant.

Brands

Shirts, socks, sodas: everything seems to have a brand. Brands also seem to spread—you have probably seen handbag firms put their names on jeans, and jeans firms put their names on handbags. Why would a firm do such a thing? It should be clear from the start that a first factor at work here is that we are not talking about firms selling products that buyers view as identical goods. If consumers cannot tell your product in any way from your competitors' products, you won't brand it because branding is clearly not costless—you have to pay for legal rights, pay for labels, pay for advertising, pay to stop infringement of your brand, and on and on. A producer who tries to brand in a market where consumers view all products as completely identical will have higher costs and quickly be priced out of the market by firms who don't pay for branding.

Since branding costs money, firms that do it must expect to get something out of it. That something is consumer loyalty—so when you need a facial tissue you buy Kleenex, or when you need aspirin you reach for Bayer. Now why would consumers do such a thing? Clearly, you are paying firms to cover their branding costs, or otherwise they wouldn't push their brands. As a customer, are you just being a fool, manipulated by advertising to pay for brands that mean essentially nothing?

The answer, actually, is no. You are getting something substantial when you buy a brand. One thing you get is an assurance of consistency in quality. A second is the pleasure of being seen by others using the brand. Effective brands, in other words, carry information. They tell you, as the buyer, something about the qualities of the good you are buying, and they tell others around you something about your personal qualities and character. Let's look at these two features of brands separately.

A good way to appreciate the quality assurance dimension of brands is to think about your last trip driving cross-country when you passed through a strange town during lunch hour. You needed to get something to eat to keep going. Now you knew from experience in your hometown that there must certainly be two or three really great eateries that the locals go to because they get great food at a good price. You also knew from experience that there were a bunch of local restaurants where sitting down to lunch may well cause you deep regret a little farther down the road. There was also a McDonald's on the corner.

Now, where did you choose to eat on your trip? It would be a good bet that you walked through the golden arches rather than took a chance on a place you knew nothing about. Why would you pick the familiar branded product over those you did not know? The answer should be clear. You went to McDonald's because you knew what you were getting. You had confidence about exactly the level of quality you would get in the food you bought.

That is one thing that effective brands give consumers—an assurance of consistency in quality. When goods are not identical in markets, there is an information gap about quality, and brands attempt to close that gap. When you need to buy a product that you have not purchased before, one option is that you can research the possibilities by consulting past issues of *Consumer Reports*. Another is that you can buy a trusted brand. That's why wise brand-holders go to all the trouble they do to enforce uniform standards on their suppliers. As a consumer you only have confidence in a brand as long as it meets your expectations. One bad experience is enough to lose you forever. That is why, if they are sensible, when a company with a brand finds their reputation under attack they will go to extremes to prove their commitment to quality. You may recall episodes in recent years of tampering with pain medications, tainted meat in fast-food restaurants, and impure ingredients in sodas. In these cases, to protect their reputation, brand-holders took drastic measures to reassure consumers about the quality of their products. They cleared the shelves and threw millions of dollars of product away. In cases where firms were slow to act or cursory in their efforts, they received severe criticism that hurt them badly (and cost key executives their jobs).

A study by Bart Bronnenberg, Sanjay Dhar, and Jean-Pierre Dubé of thirty-four consumer product industries found that brands clearly work. Their data showed that brands had persistent effects on consumer beliefs about quality.

In their sample, nationally distributed brands had market shares that were closely tied to consumer perceptions of quality. In some of the cases in the study's sample these effects had lasted for over a hundred years.

In a series of studies using well-known clothing logos, Rob Nelissen and Marijn Meijers also found that people clearly respond to brands as positive indicators of quality. In one experiment, a worker who conducted surveys at a shopping mall wore clothes with a respected logo one day and identical clothes without a logo the next. When she wore the logo, 52 percent of the people she approached agreed to take the survey. When she did not wear the logo, only 13 percent of those approached agreed. In another experiment, people watched videos of a man being interviewed for a job. In one video he wore a shirt with a logo, and in the second he did not. Those watching the video where the logo appeared rated the man more highly as a candidate for the job. In another experiment, two women went door-to-door collecting for charity wearing logo and nonlogo shirts on alternative days. Their collections on the logo days averaged 79 percent higher than when wearing identical clothes without logos.

The fact that a brand with a well-established reputation for quality has these effects explains why the handbag makers try to put their names on jeans and the jeans makers on handbags. This has to be done with care, however, or the brand will lose its value as information about product quality. There is no quicker way to kill a brand than to put it on low-quality merchandise or allow it to be used in ways to fool or mislead customers.

One of the issues faced by brands as improvements in communication technology have spread among consumers is that buyers now have much greater access to sources of information about products. Recall the example we gave of stopping at McDonald's for lunch when you were driving through a strange town during lunch hour. You made that choice because you knew what you were getting at McDonald's but not at the local eateries. Now suppose you can turn on your smartphone as you pass through the town, ask "Where's a good place to eat?," and get an immediate list of rankings and reviews. Will you stop at McDonald's now?

The message for you as a consumer in dealing with everyday prices and markets is that buying a brand will cost you money but that you are getting something for that cash. The main purpose of a brand is an assurance of quality, and you should consider whether that assurance of quality is worth it. You should not be too tied to a brand because alternatives may be very close in quality. Internet sources and publications like *Consumer Reports* can give you a good idea whether the extra cost of that brand name interior paint or polo shirt is worth it. You probably should be especially cautious about buying a name on goods that are outside of the home market for that brand. There is probably not much reason to believe that the people doing surveys in the shopping mall who wear shirts with well-known logos are more trustworthy or reliable than those wearing plain shirts, or that handkerchiefs with your favorite jean brand on them are particularly worth the extra cost.

These cautions all make good sense, but they ignore another thing that you get when you buy a brand. That, of course, is that you get the pleasure of being seen using the brand. This is not much of a factor in peoples' minds when it comes to buying facial tissue or furniture polish, but it can be important in buying suits or cars. The quality assurance information provided by brands addresses the structural fact that there is an information gap consumers face when buying many consumer goods. A brand can help close the information gap by telling customers that the good has objective features of safety, durability, or reliability. The demonstration information provided by brands, on the other hand, addresses a behavioral bias. A brand can tell customers that the good has subjective features of image, status, or identity.

As the discussion of fads showed, people have a strong tendency to care about what others are thinking and doing. One way of connecting to others in this way is through the goods people choose to buy. People tend to have a list in mind of the kinds of cars they will drive, the clothes they will wear, and the places they will live. Consumption decisions are made in a social context, and they are part of the actions people take to show their identity and character. Brands can be used to take advantage of this behavioral bias by implying that goods indicate that their users have desired traits.

A branded good, then, can carry both objective and subjective information. Since branded goods cost more money, the decision you have to make is whether this information is worth the cost. In many cases it will be. When you travel, it may make excellent sense to stay and eat at hotels and restaurants with trusted brands. When you buy goods like auto tires or lawn mowers where safety and reliability are a central issue, the same may well apply. If the image conveyed by wearing a certain brand of watch or carrying a certain handbag is important to you, then the same may be true. The key point is to be aware of these effects and think about them as you make consumption decisions. Be sure to use consumer reviews to check that the objective qualities you are hoping for are actually possessed by the good, and, in particular, be wary of the use of brands that are placed on products that have not earned a deserved reputation for quality.

CHAPTER FOUR

Santa Claus, Ticket Scalping, and Gift Cards

Information Gaps in Everyday Markets

As we have just seen, fashion, fads, and brands are features of everyday markets that exist in large part because of information gaps between buyers and sellers. In some cases it is information that buyers do not know about sellers that matters—creating the opportunities for fads and brands—and sometimes it is information that sellers do not know about buyers, as in fashion goods. As these examples suggest, information gaps and their effects are one of the more important structural features contributing to patterns in everyday markets and prices. Since information gaps are common in consumer markets, it is worth spending more time looking at other examples. In particular, the existence of these gaps in one form or another turns out to be critical in explaining the trends and patterns we see in buying gifts, ticket scalping, and the market for gift cards.

Santa Claus

Gift buying can be such a pain. I am hardly ever sure if I am getting something that will be appreciated, and I certainly don't want to give something that might be seen as off-putting. If you think about it a minute, it is clear that gift buying has an important structural difference from the normal type of market transaction. In most market sales, the person buying the product is the one who will use it. In gift buying, however, the person picking and paying for the product is not the user. The information gap in gift giving, in other words, is not between the buyer and the seller, but between the buyer and the user of the good.

I will use Santa Claus here to represent the giving of gifts. Christmas is not the only gift-giving occasion that is common in the United States, of course; you may give gifts for Hanukkah, Kwanzaa, birthdays, weddings, baby showers, anniversaries, and retirements all in the same (very expensive) month. Balancing it all out (hopefully) is the fact that you receive gifts as well. But you probably have noticed a regularity here. You know what dear Aunt Sally pays for that new blouse from Nordstrom she gives you each year, but it is never quite "you." So you always exchange it or add it to the "never-wear collection" at the back of your closet. In fact, it seems that most gifts you get are not quite worth to you what you know people paid for them. Your distant Great-Aunt Ruth, however, avoids this problem by always sending cash. You know that it is probably true as well that the people you give gifts to often find what you give them to be "not really worth it"—it is always a burden to buy something for Uncle Raúl, for example, because you don't know what he wants. This pattern is so common that it seems there must be something regular going on here.

Joel Waldfogel of Yale University had the same experience you have had with gift giving; gifts never seem to be quite worth to the receiver what the buyer paid for them. So he decided to survey students in his classes during January and March about the prices of the holiday gifts given to them in December. These prices were then compared to the value the students personally put on the gifts they received. In his first survey of student values, Waldfogel found a difference in the two values of one-tenth to one-third, which he called the value of the gifts that was destroyed by giving. In a second student survey with a larger and broader sample, Waldfogel found the same result, with an average discount of about 10 percent.

What creates this divergence in value? Gift giving is distinctive in two essential ways. First, in normal market transactions there is no difference between the value placed on a purchased product by the buyer and the user of the good because they are the same person. Gift giving, however, requires by definition a divergence between the buyer and the user. This actually would not be a problem if it was not for the second central distinctive feature of gift giving. This factor is the problem of imperfect information that we first met in the used car market. In this case, the lack of information that creates a problem is between the gift giver and gift receiver. You can't really know how Uncle Raúl values that new tie you just bought. You may get him something he really likes, but most likely you will error in the direction of giving something that he values less than the equivalent amount of cash.

If lack of information is what creates the problem in gift giving, a couple of implications would seem to follow. Say that your birthday is next week and that you always get one gift from your boyfriend and one from your Aunt Sally whom you talk to once every five years. Who is more likely to give you cash, and who will more likely give you a gift that you value very close to its cash price? It seems sensible that those who are closest to you—your boyfriend in this case—will know just what to get. Those who are distant from you will be more likely to give you gifts you don't value much, or, to avoid the problem of giving you something you have no interest in, just give cash.

Joel Waldfogel surveyed his students about these possibilities as well, and this is exactly what he found. As a measure of the relation between the cash value of gifts and the value put on them by receivers, he collected data on how often gifts were exchanged. His sample showed just what you would expect; fewer exchanges were made of gifts given by people closest to the receiver. In his initial sample, between 6 and 7 percent of noncash gifts from siblings and friends were exchanged, 10 percent of the gifts were exchanged from parents, 13 percent from grandparents, and 21 percent from aunts and uncles. You would expect just the opposite percentages for cash gifts, with those farthest from close connections to the receiver tending to give cash more often. This is also what Waldfogel found: cash gifts as a percentage of total gifts were 42 percent from grandparents, 14 percent from aunts and uncles, 10 percent from parents, and 6 percent from siblings and friends.

If there is this demonstrable and consistent gap on average between physical gifts and their cash value to the recipient—and we have all probably had the experience of getting gifts from a well-meaning relative that somehow never hit the mark—then why do people persist in the practice? Waldfogel and others who have puzzled over gift giving suggest several possibilities, including that there is a sentimental value attached to gift giving that matters, that gift giving is a signal to the receiver of the gift that the giver cares about their relationship, and that gifts are usually given in the context of a cultural celebration that creates identity within a community. As an experienced gift giver and receiver, you know these features very well. As you probably said when you put Aunt Sally's latest gift in the back of the closet, "It was really nice of Auntie to remember me." Another factor that seems also to be at work is an emotional stigma attached to giving cash in a transaction that is connected with a highly personal relationship.

The fact that there can be a sentimental value attached to gift giving for both the giver and the receiver can in some cases reinforce the problem of buying a gift the recipient values highly. A study of Valentine gifts by Adelle Yang and Oleg Urminsky found that men tended to buy a dozen roses in full bloom over two dozen rose buds about to bloom, even though the recipients preferred the buds. The reason appeared to be a difference in the immediate emotional response the gifts solicited, with men responding to the fact that the blossoms received more effusive hugs and smiles than the buds.

Gifts, then, are an excellent example of "price-plus" goods like the candy bar described earlier. In this case the "plus" includes not only the time implied by searching for an appropriate gift but also the nature of the giver and the particular circumstances of the gift. The best gifts combine both a monetary value to the receiver that is close to the market value plus a high sentimental and relationship value. Sometimes the simplest and least expensive of gifts can be the most valued, if the sentiment attached is meaningful. I still have a pack of football cards my father brought home to me when I was young and quite ill because he gave it to me at a moment when the thought and care it reflected meant a lot.

It might be noted in passing that the same problem—a difference between the buyer and user of a good and a lack of perfect information between the giver and the receiver—applies to government benefit-in-kind programs. A study by Eugene Smolensky and several colleagues found the same pattern of "value destruction" in public housing, Medicare, and Medicaid programs as did Waldfogel in gift giving. They also found, as you might expect, no value loss for food stamp or rent subsidy programs, which are benefits that are very close to cash. Interestingly, the losses as a percentage of market value were no larger and often smaller for government benefit-in-kind programs than for holiday gift giving. Although Smolensky and his colleagues did not consider it, one difference we can be pretty confident exists between government benefit-in-kind and personal gifts is that the sentimental value people attach to the government "gifts" is likely to be smaller.

Ticket Scalping

Scalping is that common activity you become most aware of when you forgot to buy those promised tickets two months ago for you and your favorite nephew to go to the sold-out big game. All you can do is search Internet sites or show up at the game and look around for some guy named Al who has two great seats "right behind" the home-team bench that he is offering to sell—at a premium, of course. To most people, there seems to be something nasty about scalpers. The ticket price should be the ticket price. It seems that someone must be being taken advantage of somewhere in the deal. Because many people think scalping is wrong, many cities and states outlaw it. Officials at the 2012 London Olympics went to a great deal of trouble to try to control it. The 2016 Better Online Ticket Sales Act in the United States added federal controls to the practice. Yet scalping continues to survive and thrive, and it is clear that it can serve a useful purpose (it saved the day, after all, for you and your nephew). What is going on with scalping and why does it exist?

Ticket scalping occurs when you purchase a ticket for an event you want to see at a price above its face value from someone who already bought the ticket. Now, immediately this looks like a strange thing to have to do. If you want to buy a new book by your favorite author, you don't buy a copy at above the marked price from a current owner. You go to a store and buy your own copy at the regular price. The same goes for new cars, or shoes, or that espresso machine you covet for the empty corner in your kitchen. Something different from normal markets must be going on for scalping to exist.

The answer, of course, is the fact that you cannot go down to the box office and buy a ticket at the face value. When all the tickets are gone, your only hope is to get a ticket from someone who already owns one. Now you might have a good buddy who has an extra seat for the event who will sell you the ticket at face value, but quite often your only choice is to buy a ticket from someone who bought that ticket in the first place only because they wanted to resell it at a profit.

The fundamental structural factor at work in ticket scalping is our now familiar situation of a lack of perfect information. If information were perfect, people who schedule performances would charge the price (or set of prices— all seats are not the same, after all) that would result in exactly the available number of seats being sold for every performance. This task is particularly difficult for performance halls and stadiums because they are usually quite limited in their ability to adjust the number of seats for sale. They may be able to add or subtract a few hundred seats by reconfiguring the space, but basically the number of tickets for sale is close to a fixed amount. Since they cannot adjust the number of seats for sale, they have to focus on the price per seat. So you will see in the same concert hall that some performers have seats sold for $25 and still have a third of the seats empty, while other performers at the same place have seats for sale for $500 each and scalpers at work outside the door.

The fact that information is imperfect also suggests why tickets are often priced at lower than possible levels. A string of sellouts attracts more favorable attention than a series of partially empty performances. This becomes part of the information that people use to judge the quality of the performance offered. In order to create this valuable information, ticket sellers may be willing to underprice tickets a bit today in order to sell more tickets tomorrow.

In a detailed look at the problems facing ticket sellers, Pascal Courty found that another fundamental problem in ticket sales was differences between ticket buyers. Some buyers know far ahead of time that they want to attend an event, and they make their purchases accordingly. Others, however, only discover that they are able or want to attend an event much closer to its date. This can happen for many reasons. Perhaps there is a change in a personal schedule— for example, someone who thought they were going to be out of town on the event day has that trip canceled—or it could be due to intervening events making attendance more attractive, like a thirty-game winning streak by the hometown team. Ticket sellers need to accommodate their early customers who value planning and assured seating. If they do not have a way to charge late buyers prices that reflect the scarcity of seating as the event approaches or to stop secondhand sales of tickets, then scalpers can prosper.

As a result, it is not unusual to find a situation where ticket prices turn out to be underpriced and where scalpers are at work. What role do they play in this market? Clearly, what scalpers do is try to take advantage of the underpricing. If scalpers do their work perfectly, they will set the price that would just make the number of buyers and sellers exactly equal. They obviously cannot do this precisely, but they do their best to capture all they can of the extra money that tickets could have sold for that the original ticket sellers were not able to take.

Who loses and who gains in this process? It might seem that the original ticket seller loses a lot to the scalper. It is true that the scalper is getting money that may have gone to the original seller, but actually the original seller may be getting something for the money they are not receiving. The fact of a sell-out and active scalping buys the original seller favorable publicity, which may pay off quite well in the future. So the original seller may not lose much in the process.

If the original seller feels scalper prices are too high compared to the original ticket price, the original seller may be able to adjust ticket prices upward—just ask recent buyers of Super Bowl tickets how this works. Another option is for the original seller to get into the reselling business himself—this is what the recent proliferation of concert and sports Internet resale sites is all about. Or the original seller can try to come up with a technique to charge early and late buyers different prices. Changes in the technology of selling tickets have allowed original sellers to try several possibilities to do this. Some baseball teams, for example, have experimented with holding tickets back and creating online auctions to sell these tickets as game time nears. Some teams and some concert promoters are moving to allow the price of all tickets to vary based on demand. New technology can be used by scalpers as well as by ticket sellers, however. The 2016 Better Online Ticket Sales Act in the United States aims at controlling "bots" by scalpers (high-speed buying software) that override the buying limits on seller websites. A scalper in 2014 used a bot to buy 1,000 U2 concert tickets in less than a minute despite the four-ticket per customer limit on the website. Ticketmaster reports that bots made five billion attempts to buy tickets on its site in 2016.

Any possible loss to the original seller, however, is not what makes most people upset about scalping. The part they don't like about scalping is that they have to pay $100 for a ticket that they could have had for only $50. So it seems that the scalper is taking something away from the final buyer.

Is this true? Yes, it is. Some people really want to see the performance, so they are willing to pay $100 a ticket to go. If they only had to pay $50 for a ticket, they would have got a very good deal. If they are true die-hard fans, even at the $100 they have to pay a scalper they may still be paying less than they would have been willing to if they had to; it is just that the deal is not as good as it would have been at $50 a ticket. So the scalper is taking some of this "good deal" away.

It seems at first glance that the scalper does something here that is not acceptable and that does not exist in other markets. A little reflection shows, however, that this is not true. Even in markets where the number of goods desired just equals the amount offered for sale at the market price, almost all of the individuals who buy the product get a "good deal" at the market price. Almost everyone would have been willing to pay something more for the good (some people will be paying their exact value of the good). Those who would have been willing to pay more are happy that they only had to pay what they did. In a market of voluntary transactions, it can't be true that buyers thought the good was worth less than they paid for it; if that was the case—if they thought the price was not a "good deal" for them—they wouldn't buy the good. One fact that is often missed in thinking about this "good deal" on the buy-er's side is that in markets where buying and selling are done without restraint the "good deal" is realized by sellers as well. "Good deals" are actually the norm in all market transactions. The existence of "good deals" on both sides, and of both sides of the transaction trying to get the best of the deal for them-selves, is present in every voluntary market transaction.

Scalpers charging more than the face value of tickets to willing buyers, then, are not doing something "unnatural" that does not occur in other mar-kets. All buyers and sellers try to capture for themselves as much of the "good deal" the other side is receiving. When they underprice their tickets, how-ever, original ticket sellers give up part of the buyer's side "good deal," which would be theirs at higher prices. Scalpers take advantage of this opportunity by trying to capture for themselves part of the money that the original ticket sellers are giving up.

This is how buyers of tickets lose to scalpers; the scalpers make them pay for a part of the "good deal" they would have gotten if they had bought the ticket at its face value. This is what most people object to about scalping; it does not seem right that their potential good deal gets captured by someone else. This attitude, however, overlooks the positive service that scalpers pro-vide. After all, if it wasn't for the scalper, you couldn't take your nephew to the game at all. And since you are free to decide that the scalper's price is too high to be worth it, if you buy the ticket that must mean that you are still getting what seems to you to be a good deal.

So, who in the end gains and who loses? The original ticket seller loses some potential income but gains the favorable attention of a sold-out house. Those who were lucky enough to get tickets at the underpriced amount get a better deal than they would have received if they had bought the ticket at the higher price where the number of seats demanded just equaled the number for sale. People who buy tickets from scalpers lose some of the "good deal" they would have had if they could have bought a ticket at the underpriced amount, but scalping allows them to go to an event they really want to see, and since they voluntarily buy the ticket they still must find it to be a good deal. Scalpers gain the difference between the price they paid for their tickets and the price they receive for the ones they sell (taking on, as they do so, the risk of not being able to get rid of all the tickets they bought) and provide a useful service to those who really want to see the event but were not able to get tickets at the original price.

How does it all come out at the end? From one point of view, it seems that the people you really should be irritated at are not the scalpers but those who were able to get the original underpriced tickets and who attended the event. They got extra gains at no extra cost or risk and didn't provide any service of value in return. Fundamentally, though, the real problem is the fact that the tickets were underpriced and not the scalping. Because they want to sell tickets early to people who want them, sellers cannot wait until the last minute to judge the ideal ticket price. In such a situation, the sellers want to error on the side of underpricing in order to better guarantee a sellout. The underpricing gap between the ticket price and the price that would make the number of seats demanded equal to the number for sale creates the opportunity for someone other than the original ticket seller to capture some of the money that buyers are willing to pay. Scalping is an inevitable outcome in such a situation.

So, what can you do? If you know you have a good chance to attend the event, you should take advantage of the early sale period. This is a particularly good idea if there is a well-developed resale market that you can use if it turns out that you cannot attend the event. A friend of mine, for example, buys season tickets to the football games of his favorite college and takes advantage of the university-sponsored resale market for those he can't use. Since the team has done well the last few years, he has actually come out ahead on the deal. If, however, you can't plan ahead and take advantage of the initial ticket price, then you can resort yourself to the sponsored resale market or talk to that guy named Al who has those great tickets. You may lose some of the extra gain you would gain from paying the underpriced value of the ticket, but you will get to make your nephew happy and enjoy the game.

Gift Cards

You know all about gift cards, of course, because you have bought and received them. You probably know that they have not been around forever, but that they have become popular and that they provide the flexibility of being close to cash for purchases. When you buy one, however, you may have wondered if a card is not quite personal enough as a gift.

Jennifer Pate Offenberg was interested in the rising popularity of gift cards as well and decided to investigate the trends and issues they create. Gift certificates, of course, have been around for decades, but the first gift card using a magnetic strip appeared in 1995. By 2007 the total value of sales in the

United States using gift cards had risen to nearly $80 billion. Offenberg found that magnetic strip cards are popular with firms because they have lower costs to issue and to process than paper gift certificates. She also found that they have become increasingly acceptable among consumers because they are seen as more personal than giving cash. According to a 2004 survey of consumer preferences, giving gift cards was preferred to giving cash by a 2 to 1 margin.

It would seem that gift cards provide a nice solution to the gift-giving dilemma identified by Joel Waldfogel in his survey about the values students put on holiday gifts that they received. You will recall from our earlier discussion that Waldfogel found that the gap in information between the giver and user of a gift caused the average nonmonetary holiday gift to be valued by the recipient from a tenth to a third below the actual price paid for it. Since cards are close to cash, it would seem that this gap would barely or not even exist for gift cards. To test for this, Offenberg collected data on eBay auctions for gift cards. Surprisingly, she found that a significant gap still existed between the dollar value on the card and its sale price. In fact, taking everything she could think of into account, the gap was about the same as Waldfogel found for physical gifts, from 15 to 20 percent.

Given this overall result, Offenberg then looked for other patterns of interest in the eBay auctions of gift cards. She found there was a significant difference in the discount between types of firms, with home improvement stores like Home Depot and discount stores like Walmart having low discounts of about 10 percent or so. At the other extreme, apparel and jewelry stores had larger discounts on the order of 20 percent. The differences that seemed to matter were the national distribution of stores, large size, and the variety of products being sold. She also found a significant difference in discounts based on the value of the gift card. Small value cards had low discounts, while large value cards had the highest discounts.

The same patterns were found by *Consumer Reports* in an article that reviewed online sites that will buy gift cards that you don't want. The lower discounts again were for places like Walmart and Home Depot, with larger discounts for specialty stores like Brooks Brothers. In the *Consumer Reports* sample, the range of prices offered was from 50 percent to 90 percent of the face value of the cards.

The message for gift shopping seems clear. Gift cards are seen as more personal gifts than cash. But they have the same tendency as physical gifts to be discounted by their recipients. If you want to give a card and reduce the discount, you should buy one for less than $50 at a large, national, broad-product-offering store. Offenberg found that gift cards at consumer electronics stores had an average discount in her eBay sample of about 15 percent. The ultimate message, unfortunately, is that although they are convenient, gift cards do not ideally solve the problem created by the gap in information between the giver and the recipient of a gift.

CHAPTER FIVE

Bait-and-Switch, Counterfeit Goods, and Low-Price Guarantees

How Sellers Can Take Advantage of Information Gaps

The price and market patterns in gift giving and ticket scalping created by information gaps between buyers and sellers can be a cause of anxiety. You probably don't want to check your blood pressure right after completing a last-minute scalping transaction or after spending hours searching for what you hope is that ideal graduation gift for your niece. When you have to deal with the stress of buying that last-minute birthday gift or that last-minute ticket to a great event, however, you can perhaps take solace in knowing that information gaps in markets can lead to situations that are actually worse. At least gift giving and ticket scalping don't involve deception. Given the opportunities that information gaps create, it shouldn't be a surprise to learn that firms in some markets will try to do exactly that. Having to pay an above-list price to a ticket scalper is bad enough, but irritation reaches an entirely new level when a seller tries to take advantage of an information gap to fool you or lie to you.

Bait-and-Switch

Bait-and-switch advertising is lying. This is the practice where a firm advertises an incredible deal on a product to attract customers, but when they show up they find that the last item at that special price has just been sold and they are offered instead another that is similar but at a higher price. The interesting thing about bait-and-switch advertising is that it is a readily discoverable lie. Once customers are in the store, they know that the ad was misleading. Now this would seem a strange thing for a firm to do. Some customers who are attracted by the ad who find themselves getting the "we-just-sold-the-last-one-at-that-price-but-have-a-slightly-more-expensive-one-right-here" routine will get mad, stomp out of the place, bad-mouth the store to their friends, and maybe even call the Better Business Bureau or write a critical online review. Why not just tell the truth and avoid this potential hassle?

Edward Lazear was puzzled by the obvious lying involved in the bait-and-switch and looked in detail at what is going on here. Lazear concluded that a special combination of structural factors has to exist in a market to make using the bait-and-switch profitable.

The first required feature, according to Lazear, is that the products involved in the bait-and-switch must be differentiated, although quite close substitutes. Using Lazear's example, a bait-and-switch strategy trying to get customers to move from a minivan to a $750,000 Lamborghini is not going to work. Moving customers from a basic minivan to one with tinted windows and pinstriping for $750 more is much more likely to succeed.

Given this foundation, the next essential structural element for bait-and-switch to be profitable is that there must be more customers for the advertised good than for the actual good available. This is necessary because some people who are attracted by the ad will get mad and stomp out; the firm will inevitably lose some of the customers that come through the door because of its misleading advertising. The most important structural factor, however, is the existence of imperfect information in the market. If there wasn't an information gap, people would not be fooled by misleading ads. Imperfect information is at the heart of bait-and-switch advertising.

Another way that imperfect information matters for the bait-and-switch to work is that customers must incur costs in order to find information about the good being advertised. These costs include, for example, the effort it takes to find and read ads and the time it takes to drive across town to the store. Once the customer has been attracted by the bait-and-switch ad and is in the door, he has a choice. He can walk out in a huff and start searching again for the good he wants, or he can look "at that nice one over here that is really close to the one in the ad." Given the difference in the search costs between these two options, the customer may well choose to examine the offered good. The level of these search costs to the consumer, then, is critical in a successful bait-and-switch. If the search costs for alternatives elsewhere are low, too many of the customers attracted by the ad will walk out the door. If the search costs are basically zero—say by readily checking alternatives on the smartphone in your pocket—then all ads will be truthful. There will be no possibility for the bait-and-switch to work because all customers will walk out of the store and look for another product elsewhere. If these search costs are high, however, many of the customers attracted by the ad will stay and look at the goods really available for sale.

Since the only reason to try the bait-and-switch is to make greater profits, Lazear concludes that one last structural feature is necessary for the strategy to work. There must be low costs to show customers the goods available once they arrive at the store. The whole idea of bait-and-switch is to attract a lot of customers. Once they arrive, they must be talked to, shown around, and sold the goods actually available. This takes time and effort, some of which will be wasted because some people will not go for the switch. If this wasted time and effort is too expensive, then the bait-and-switch fails to achieve its ultimate purpose, and the firm will be better off by truthful advertising.

The end result is that quite a collection of structural factors is necessary for bait-and-switch advertising to work. Markets having these features are not uncommon, however, as any dedicated American consumer is well aware. Despite federal and state laws attempting to control blatant use of the practice, it does not take too much shopping experience in the United States to find out that "you are just ten minutes too late to get the last one offered at our advertised price." If you come across such a situation, the best strategy is to accept the reality that you have been drawn in by a lie, take a deep breath, and weigh your options. You have the choice of walking across the showroom to take a look at that other item that is "just like" the one you wanted, walking out the door and continuing your search for the good elsewhere, or going home and not buying the product at all. Buying the actually available good in the showroom or continuing your search elsewhere will cost you more than you had hoped when you read the ad. If that extra cost is too high, then the best choice is just to go home. All are viable options, and the one that is best will depend on the extra costs you face from looking elsewhere or accepting the good that "is just like" the one that was advertised.

Counterfeit Goods

You know about counterfeit goods. You are sure there is something questionable about the Rolex watches offered by the guy who sells out of the back of his van down the block from the supermarket. You are just as suspicious about the Levis and Gucci purses he offers next to the watches. (You also have questions about the advertised freshness of the produce at the supermarket, but that is another story.)

It is clear that counterfeit goods clearly will not exist in markets with perfect information. If information is accurate and complete, customers will not be fooled by sellers offering goods that are not what they claim to be. It is the structural factor of imperfect information faced by consumers in markets with differentiated products that creates the opportunity for counterfeiting. These circumstances come together to create a larger issue than you might expect. According to a report on counterfeiting in *The Economist* magazine, an early 2000s survey estimated that 7–9 percent of all world trade involved counterfeit goods. Another study from the same time period estimated that U.S. firms lost $200–$250 billion a year to counterfeiters. A 2008 article in the *Los Angeles Times* estimated the annual value of total world trade in illegitimate goods at $600 billion.

Something more than a lack of information among consumers and the existence of differentiated products is generally required to motivate counterfeiters, however. Counterfeiters tend to focus on high-margin brand names. Since counterfeiting is illegal and thus a risky business, there is not much reason to produce fake low-price, low-profit, mass-produced goods. The big money in counterfeiting is in high-priced, restricted-supply goods with widely recognized brands, although specialized niche markets can be at risk as well. In the late 2010s, indigenous dressmakers in southern Mexican villages found that their designs were so popular that they had to deal with counterfeits of their distinctive patterns.

All of this seems quite straightforward, but there is a less obvious dimension to the issue of counterfeit goods. Consider who is hurt by counterfeits. Certainly, the producers of authentic goods are harmed. They lose sales; they lose their reputation for producing excellent goods if counterfeiting is rampant and of low quality; and the extra supply of nonauthentic goods drives down prices. There are clearly not any redeeming features of counterfeiting for real-brand producers, except perhaps for the dubious honor of being chosen as important enough to counterfeit.

For consumers, however, the story is different. In a study of counterfeit goods, Richard Higgins and Paul Rubin found that the motivation of consumers matters in determining the nature of counterfeit markets. They found that consumers who buy brand names because the trademark signifies objective quality features like safety, reliability, and durability are usually hurt when they buy counterfeit goods. Counterfeits are almost always inferior to the actual product and are offered for sale at a significant discount off full price. Counterfeiters do not worry about the reputation of their goods. These costs are borne by the authentic producers. Consumers who value objective quality features that are lured in by the low price offered by the counterfeiter are harmed because they do not get the good they expect.

Some consumers, however, do not buy the good for its objective qualities. As you will recall from our earlier discussion of brands, some customers are most concerned about the subjective qualities of a label that are reflected in the fact that they are able to display their use of goods with that brand name. It is enough for them to be seen wearing that Rolex watch or carrying that

Gucci bag. If the objective qualities of craft and skill in construction are not reflected in the good, they don't really care. In fact, they may well know the good is a fake and buy it anyway, just to be able to display the brand.

Counterfeiting has a different effect on these consumers. They get to display the brand they want at a cut rate, so they are not hurt by counterfeiting like consumers who buy the brand for its objective qualities. The existence of these different kinds of consumers is important because of its implications for the extent of counterfeiting. If both consumers and producers are hurt by counterfeiting, the pressure to detect and punish people offering faked goods will be more intense. If consumers do not care whether the goods are counterfeit or not, however, only the producers will press for counterfeit controls. If only the producers care and the consumers are indifferent, the potential gains will be higher and the risks lower for counterfeiters, and one would expect more counterfeiting to exist. The behavioral motivation behind brand buying by consumers, then, will be an important factor determining the extent of counterfeiting.

Counterfeiters, then, would seem to face ideal conditions when consumers buy brands for display value alone. The consumers do not care about objective qualities, so they won't complain about shoddy workmanship. The producers are hurt, but they don't have outraged consumers backing up their demands for action. It would seem that counterfeiters could act almost with impunity in such conditions.

On further reflection, however, it is evident that conditions are not as ideal as they may seem, especially in the case of goods bought primarily for display purposes. These consumers do experience some harm from counterfeiting, even if they are indifferent to the objective quality of the good they buy. The reason these consumers are buying the good in the first place is because of the snob appeal of displaying a prestige good. Counterfeiting increases the supply of the good, however, making it more common and reducing its exclusivity. The active buying of counterfeit goods for show purposes will reduce the value of the display. The ease of selling counterfeit goods to consumers who want them for show purposes, then, may not be as great an advantage to the counterfeiter as it seems. Too-active counterfeiting can destroy the market for the consumer, the authentic producer, and the counterfeiter.

In order to avoid the costs of their markets being harmed by fake goods, firms that have to deal with active counterfeiting can take action. In a study of shoe producers in China, where firms faced severe counterfeiting activities, Yi Qian found that firms adopted four strategies that were effective in reducing counterfeit sales: innovation focused on product qualities that were difficult to copy; setting up licensed retail stores to control final sales; creating internal brand protection offices to monitor the market; and actively cooperating with government agencies to set up and enforce counterfeiting laws. In his sample of shoe firms, prices had fallen when counterfeiting began because customers perceived that quality had been reduced. After firms invested in the strategies to reduce counterfeiting, shoe prices rose strongly, on average 45 percent over two years. Over the same period nonbranded shoe prices rose slightly and counterfeit shoe prices remained at a constant level. Qian interpreted these price changes as evidence that the measures worked. Given that counterfeiting can have clear negative consequences for consumers and producers, it is comforting to know that there are strategies that seem to be effective in limiting its effects.

Low-Price Guarantees

You have probably seen a sign in a store window or read an ad that in bright colors and large font screams "Low-Price Guarantee!!" If you went into the store to ask about it, the helpful clerk probably explained that the store policy is one of two versions of the scheme. One version is to guarantee a buyer the best price that is offered to any customer in the thirty days or so following the purchase. If the item goes on sale in that period, for example, you could bring your receipt back and get the difference as a refund. The second version is that the store will meet or beat the lowest price offered by a set of competitors. After you heard the explanation, you probably thanked the clerk kindly for the information—she was actually helpful and pleasant—and decided to think about it for a while. You also may have wondered about that price guarantee. Is there something special going on here? Why do they do that?

Low-price guarantees sound like a strategy by firms to draw in customers by being more competitive in the prices they charge. According to Don Waldman and Elizabeth Jensen in their analysis of such practices, however, low-price guarantees can be a strategy used by firms to reduce competition and thus avoid lower prices. According to Waldman and Jensen, firms want to stay away from price competition whenever they can. The ideal result is if they are the only seller in a market with no potential entrants. With a protected monopoly, they can pick the price that will maximize the profit that they make. The problem that competition creates for firms is that multiple sellers can cause this price and thus profits to fall.

One result of firms' efforts to avoid competition is a continual contest over laws affecting businesses. Consumer advocates fight for legislation that creates competitive market conditions (antitrust laws that prohibit firm actions such as price fixing, for example, or regulatory laws that require certain actions by firms such as allowing cable TV firms to provide telephone service). Firms, on the other hand, fight just as hard for rules that can avoid these outcomes (import restrictions that keep out foreign competitors, for example, or licensing requirements that raise barriers to the entry of new providers of services).

Another strategy that firms can use to help avoid competitive outcomes is simply to agree with other firms not to compete. In the United States most such explicit agreements between firms are illegal. Firms cannot, for example, sit down with direct competitors and talk about the prices they will charge and the outputs they will produce. People who work in industries covered by antitrust legislation know very well the restrictions and penalties mandated by the laws. A cousin of mine who worked in sales in the paper industry, for example, had to attend regular "Sherman Act Workshops," which went over the rules and regulations. The fact that such actions are illegal doesn't stop firms from doing it, of course. Because of the money involved, acts to avoid competition are a strong temptation and, in fact, the most common antitrust case brought to the courts is about price fixing.

Since explicit agreements among competitors are illegal, firms have to be more creative in their coordination strategies. Firms cannot sign formal price fixing agreements with competitors that are enforceable in court, so they have to come up with practices that are enforced in other ways, which brings us back to low-price guarantees.

According to Waldman and Jensen, low-price guarantees can be a strategy for firms to reach an informal agreement to avoid price competition. If you think about it a minute, this makes sense. Look again at the offer of a refund if the produce goes on sale in a given time period. If a firm guarantees to all its customers that they can get the lowest price that is offered to any individual, why would the firm ever charge a lower price to anyone? The only reason to charge a lower price to a specific customer is to make the sale. It is certainly nice to make an extra sale and add the gains to total profit, but if that sale is going to require giving refunds to dozens of others, then that sale becomes very expensive. The incentive created for a firm with a low-price guarantee is not to cut the price to anyone. The beauty of this strategy from the firm's point of view is that it is self-enforcing. No contracts or explicit agreements with firms are required. A firm will not cut its price to anyone because it will hurt itself by having to give rebates to other customers. If all the firms in an industry independently adopt such a policy, it can be an effective way to avoid price competition.

The same is true for the low-price guarantee that "we will meet or beat any competitor's price." Assume all the competitors in an industry adopt this policy, all the firms have the same price at the start, and one firm cuts its price to gain more sales. What will be the effect? Customers will not swamp the sales floor of the firm with the price cut. They will instead go to their competitors and demand that "meet or beat" price guarantee. Again the price-cutting firm hurts itself, so the policy is self-enforcing and the incentive is never to cut at all.

As an illustration of their argument about the effects of low-price guarantees, Waldman and Jensen tell the story about the federal government's attempt in a 1990 law to lower the prices the federal government paid for prescription drugs through the Medicaid program. Drug companies at the time often charged large buyers of prescription drugs lower prices than Medicaid paid for the same item. In an attempt to lower the prices charged to the federal government, the 1990 law required drug companies to in effect adopt a low-price guarantee with the federal government. The result was that drug companies now had an incentive not to offer lower prices to other large buyers of the covered drugs. The law, in other words, provided the industry with a government-mandated mechanism for avoiding price competition. As a result, the average prices for branded drugs commonly sold to Medicaid patients went up and not down. For another example, a 2015 survey of British supermarkets found that the four largest chains offered a price-match guarantee, but only for prices charged by the group and not for prices charged at low-cost rivals. As the survey concluded, the advertised slogan of one chain that the price-match guarantee meant that consumers "don't have to shop around," sounded "like an effort to abate a price war and not start one." Low-price guarantees had misled their customers again.

The message for consumers from the bait-and-switch, counterfeiting, and low-price guarantees is that you shouldn't get excited or be too impressed by offers of incredible prices on premium brand-name products or will-beat-the-competition guarantees. What you should wonder when you see these offers is whether they are attempts by sellers to take advantage of the information gaps that exist between buyers and sellers. These practices can be used by unscrupulous sellers who know more about the availability or quality of goods to deceive potential customers.

Because of the deception possible in these practices, there are laws and rules about many of these actions. Counterfeiting is a crime, the bait-and-switch is controlled, and advertising has specific rules about deceptive practices. This doesn't mean that such practices don't exist, of course. Because of the money involved, the temptation to take advantage of information gaps to deceive customers is just too strong. One of my favorite deceptive advertising examples was by an auto-glass manufacturer whose TV ads showed how remarkably clear and undistorted the view was through their window glass by filming passing outdoor scenes from the inside of a car that did not have any glass at all in its windows.

Most people who deal regularly with consumer markets soon acquire a pretty good sense about how these practices work and are appropriately skeptical when they come across an offer that is too good to be true. An attitude of healthy skepticism is the best response to have when faced with these deals. With this attitude in mind, the way to act is also clear. Since the fundamental problem that creates the possibility of deception is the existence of an information gap between buyers and sellers, the best strategy is to acquire more information before you make the final decision to buy.

One possible outcome of new technologies related to the Internet and smartphones is better and quicker access to this information as soon as you need it. Ferragamo, for example, inserts radio-frequency identification tags in its shoes to tell its customers if they have been sold a fake. The bait-and-switch and price-match guarantees won't work if you can quickly know about alternatives elsewhere. Time will tell if the new technologies are effective in this way. More buyers are making good use of their smartphones when shopping, and a 2016 article surveying the issue concluded optimistically, claiming that the "new technologies will make society richer by cultivating trust." But there are cautionary tales as well. A recent law in Chile attempted to close the information gap consumers face about retail gasoline prices by requiring gas stations to post their pump prices promptly on a government website. The firms complied, but by doing so they also closed the information gap that gas stations had about their competitors' prices. The end result was much like that with low-price guarantees. A price cut by a gas station could be met by immediate computer-generated retaliation, so the incentive to cut prices was reduced. In the end, profit margins at gas stations rose by 10 percent.

CHAPTER SIX

Computer Repairs, Mortgage Loans, Hidden Fees, and Credit Cards

Products Bought from Experts and Groups of Buyers as Structural Factors

Markets where sellers try to deceive or fool you are bad enough, but in fact they are probably not the markets that people dread dealing with the most. If you really want to raise your blood pressure, then arrange your schedule so you have to spend the day seeking the advice of "experts"—from doctors, lawyers, and plumbers to taxi drivers and computer repair people. These are people who sell you a product that is individually tailored to meet your specific needs but which you know little about. These markets can create a level of anxiety with which most of us are all too familiar. Only slightly easier to deal with are markets with a range of prices where only knowledgeable buyers can figure out how to pay the lowest fees. Given what we have found so far in our discussions of prices and price patterns, it shouldn't come as a surprise to learn that information gaps between buyers and sellers play a central role in creating the issues we face in these markets. It would be nice if expert advice and knowledgeable buyer markets were infrequent experiences, but in fact most of us have to deal with them almost every day.

Computer Repairs

If you think about it a minute, it is clear that the fundamental problem with dealing with experts is our old friend asymmetric information. I well remember the first time I brought in a personal computer to have it repaired. These products and their repair services were new at the time. I only knew that the darn thing was not working right but had no idea what the problem might be.

The feeling that you can be taken advantage of is the major problem that people have in economic transactions with experts. Clearly, the essential problem is that there is a huge gap in knowledge between buyers and sellers in these markets. Since these situations are so common (and so aggravating), Uwe Dulleck and Rudolf Kerschbamer decided to see if there were any generalizations that could be made about consumer markets with these features. They found that all the problems in dealing with experts could be blamed on the structural facts of product differentiation and asymmetric information.

A special feature of expert markets is that the differences in products offered for sale are caused by the fact that there are differences in customers. When you buy a basic hamburger at a national restaurant chain, usually every customer buys an identical product (although there is always someone who holds up the line by asking for extra pickles). Differences in customers do not matter to the seller at all. When you buy in expert service markets, however, almost every customer requires something different. Almost every taxi rider needs to go somewhere different. Every car has unique repair problems based on its history and use. The services you need to take care of computer, dental, and medical problems can vary widely. It is because the customers have different problems that the products sold are different.

As a result of this difference in products caused by the specific needs of each buyer, in expert markets you need to buy two services: first, a diagnosis of the problem, and second, a remedy. An information gap between buyers and sellers exists at both the diagnosis and the remedy stages. Because of this dual imbalance of information, you can be taken advantage of at either or both levels.

According to Dulleck and Kerschbamer, these problems would not exist if the diagnosis and remedy were packaged together and if the accuracy of the remedy could be completely validated. If there is a division between the diagnosis and remedy, or if the success of the remedy cannot be adequately affirmed, then consumers are open to being exploited. When I first visited Boston and took a taxi from the airport to a downtown hotel, the division between diagnosis and remedy didn't exist. I told the driver where I wanted to go and then I let him take me there, so the diagnosis and remedy were linked. The issue in the case of the taxi ride was validating the remedy. Since I didn't know Boston, I had no way to judge the choice of route the driver took. Since new visitors to cities can be taken advantage of because they do not know the best taxi routes to take to their destinations, most cities have regulations setting or controlling these fares.

There is nothing that can be done in expert markets about the fact that different products are provided to different customers. That is the very essence of the market. There are some things that can be done, however, about the gap in knowledge at the diagnosis and remedy stages. One solution is government regulation. Because of the consumer issues in expert markets, many of these markets have controls of some kind. Doctors and dentists have to be licensed. Taxi fares and meters are monitored and controlled. Car repair garages are subject to random inspection and evaluation by government agencies. But as you well know from your experiences as a consumer, these protections are imperfect. You can always sue, of course, if you suffer damages from the remedy provided in expert markets, but that is little help in making decisions when you have to seek expert advice.

Because government regulations and legal remedies do not provide complete protection of consumers in expert markets, in large part you are on your own. There are some clear actions you can take to help with the decisions you need to make when you have to face these markets. The main strategy that stands out is that to protect yourself you are going to have to close the information gap between you and the expert in some way.

One way to do this is to spend some time personally learning about the possible solutions to your problem. With the help of all the information available on the Internet, this can be a good use of your time. You may have a friend, for example, who has become a modest expert in a medical problem they are facing by reading widely in web sources. It will also be well worth your time to get a multiple diagnosis of your problem. This can be extremely helpful, for example, when the drains back up in your house and you don't know if you need to replace the mainline out to the street or fix a connection just outside the house. If you have a computer problem, you can use the services of magazines like *Consumer Reports* or websites like Angie's List and Yelp that collect information on the experiences of people who have used similar repair services. The February 2019 edition of *Consumer Reports*, for example, provided a step-by-step process for finding a quality auto repair shop. For a visit to a dentist or a doctor you can ask everyone you know about their experiences with different providers. You will certainly want to do the same thing about a car repair garages, home repair contractors, and attorneys.

You probably know about all of this just from living in the United States and having to buy goods and services regularly in expert markets, but that doesn't make the experience any easier. These are just not fun markets to deal with. In addition to resolving to close the information gap in some way, it can also be very helpful to remember that there are two stages to the process in expert markets, the diagnosis and the remedy. It can make the process less intimidating and more manageable by breaking it down into two steps by first focusing on the diagnosis and then taking on the task of arranging for the remedy. You do not have to make both decisions at the same time or even to use the same provider. By dividing the task in this way, you can take more personal control of the process. In particular, it may make it more likely that you will follow the advice regularly given in these markets and collect more than one estimate for resolving the problem. To do the best you can for yourself, you can do this at both the diagnosis and remedy stage.

The personal experience that always comes to my mind when I deal with expert markets happened several years ago when our 1990s-era minivan needed work on its carburetor. Since the car was still fairly new at the time, I first took it to the new car dealership. The diagnosis was that the carburetor needed replacing, at a cost of parts-plus-labor at that time of over $900. I then took the car to the mechanic who took care of our older car. His diagnosis was that a spring needed to be replaced in the carburetor, at a cost of $1.50 for parts and a free 15 minutes of labor. It didn't take long for me to choose between the two options. Since that experience I don't have any trouble keeping in mind the distinction between diagnosis and remedy and the value of getting multiple estimates.

Mortgage Loans

Buying a car, a house, and a college education are about the most complex and expensive things that most of us have to do as consumers. They are expensive, so everyone pays careful attention to the price they have to pay. Beyond that, these goods cost so much money that you probably have to borrow to pay for them. As a result, you have two prices to deal with, the price of the item itself and the price you have to pay for the loan. The whole process can seem overwhelming.

The problem most of us face in buying houses, cars, and college education is that these are complicated prices that are difficult to understand. Because we only make these purchases a few times in our lives, we don't have many opportunities to learn all the details we need to know in order to get the best deal. To make it worse, in paying for these goods we have to deal with experts in the field—real estate agents, loan officers, and car salespeople—who do these deals maybe hundreds or even thousands of times in their careers. There is a major information gap here between what we know as buyers and what the sellers know about all the options, details, and possibilities that exist.

You know that you can get good advice as a buyer in these markets. There are a lot of resources you can consult. When you are considering buying a new car, for example, you know you can buy detailed reports on cars from *Consumer Reports* as well as detailed advice about how to negotiate the best possible price from a dealer. This all takes time and attention, however, and even then you know you will be at a disadvantage. Given your lack of experience and knowledge, you expect that people tend to make mistakes in these deals.

Steven Levitt was interested in how these issues worked out in buying houses. Using a data set covering nearly 100,000 home sales in Chicago, he compared the details of homes sold that were owned by real estate agents to those owned by the rest of us. In the time period his sample covered, he found that agents on average received over 3 percent more for the sale of houses they owned. Given the prices of homes, this can amount to tens of thousands of dollars. One way agents did this was by keeping their houses on the market for an average of ten days longer than for sales of homes owned by people who were not agents. The implication is pretty clear. Because we don't know how the market works, most of us don't get the best deal possible when we sell a house.

Levitt found that the main factor creating this outcome in the housing market was the structure of the commissions real estate agents earn. In the United States, agents usually get a set percentage of the sales price. If this is 6 percent, then an extra $10,000 on the sales price is only worth $600 to an agent. If an agent sells his own house for an extra $10,000, then he gets to keep the whole $10,000. The difference in the incentives is strong enough to motivate agents to get a higher price for their own homes than for those of their clients.

There are a couple of ways to get around this problem. One is to learn more about how the market works so that you counteract this incentive, and another is not to use an agent who gets paid by commission. Studies that followed up on Levitt's results have found that both strategies work. The rise in the information available on Internet sites has reduced the agents' price gap for selling their own home by about a third, and studies of home prices sold without agents or through flat-fee agents have found that homes sell for about the same price as those sold through commission agents but with, of course, lower fees. Selling a house not using an agent took longer and the process took more work, but the savings were in the tens of thousands of dollars.

If sellers have a hard time getting the best deal, then maybe things are just fine for buyers. The Levitt results imply, after all, that home prices are somewhat lower than they might be because of the way that real estate agents get paid. This is good news for buyers. However, to buy that house almost all of us will have to borrow. Susan Woodward and Robert Hall looked at this aspect of buying a home by reviewing the details of almost 9,000 loans written by mortgage brokers over a five-year period in the late 1990s through early 2000s. Brokers are intermediate agents in the home loan process, working with borrowers on one side and lenders on the other. In the period covered in their study, mortgage brokers processed more than half of all home loans. Woodward and Hall found that brokers are paid in one of three ways, by the borrower alone, by the lender alone, or by a combination of both. Borrowers can choose one of these options, with the trade-off being paying a higher interest rate on the loan in exchange for lower cash fees. The authors found, however, that borrowers paid different prices for the loans when they made different choices among these options. In the case of no-cost loans, where the borrower pays the highest interest rate and all broker fees are paid by the lender, borrowers got the best deal on their loans. In the case where borrowers picked an option where the fee was split, they did the worst. The average savings in the cost of the loan in the no-cost case was from $670 to $1,120.

After considering possible explanations, Woodward and Hall concluded that the problem for borrowers was the complexity of the trade-off between cash fees and higher interest rates. Mortgage brokers, in other words, tended to take advantage of their knowledge of the details of the process to charge more for loans from borrowers who had less understanding of loan details. This conclusion was supported by the fact that they found that borrowers from census tracts where all the adults had a college education paid significantly less for their loans, presumably because they were better able to understand the cash and interest rate trade-off. Woodward and Hall were also able to extend their analysis to loans from banks, credit unions, and savings and loans where loan officers were paid by the institution and not by the borrower or lender. Borrowers got better terms in these loans, paying on average over $1,500 less for a loan compared to using a mortgage broker.

James Lacko and Janis Pappalardo looked at another aspect of the mortgage process by interviewing people who recently had obtained a mortgage. The participants brought their loan documents in for review and were asked a variety of questions to test their understanding of the terms of their loan. When asked about costs and fees, a large percentage of the borrowers answered questions about their loans incorrectly. Half of the borrowers did not know the actual loan amount, a third did not know the interest rate they were paying, and nearly a quarter did not know how much they had actually been charged for the loan.

The message of all this seems pretty clear. Complex, infrequent purchases like buying a car, a house, or a college education create significant challenges for consumers. We lack experience and information, and we are dealing with people who often are not very concerned with giving us the best deal. The best strategy is clearly to close this information gap and become as knowledgeable as possible about the markets and pricing schemes. It is consoling to know that obtaining this information does work. A review of a several month voluntary program for prospective low- and moderate-income homebuyers in Indianapolis found that graduates of the program had much better results in terms of mortgage terms and in terms of their ability to manage their home loans than similar borrowers who did not complete the program. That's encouraging news and can help make the task of acquiring the information less painful. Just like dealing with the computer repair shop, the car repair garage, and the plumber, you are going to have to pay attention and do the work of collecting some information if you want to do well when making complex and infrequent purchases like buying a car, a house, or a college education.

Hidden Fees

As if worrying about whether you got a good deal on your mortgage loan is not enough, there was that fee the bank charged last month when you forgot to make a transfer and wrote a check that—just barely, darn it!—overdrew the account. You knew the bank had these fees, but you had little idea what they were. You remember that you got a list of fees when you opened an account at the bank, and you seem to recall getting an update in an email at one time, but the number of fees was too overwhelming to pay much attention to. Why isn't there clearer information about those fees? Couldn't they at least warn customers when they are getting close to being penalized?

In, possibly, thinking about their own hidden bank fees, Xavier Gabaix and David Laibson looked at a variety of markets that had fees and charges that were not openly shared with their customers. Bank fees were one example, but Gabaix and Laibson found that similar situations existed with the cost of ink cartridges that go with printers and with add-on fees charged by hotels. A 2018 study of cable TV fees in Massachusetts found that added fees raised advertised prices by 40 percent and forced customers to pay up to $240 to cancel service packages they found they could not afford. In the case of one computer printer manufacturer, Gabaix and Laibson found printing cost information to be so difficult to find that it was nearly invisible to the potential buyer. They found detailed information online for all the features of the printer except for the key factor of cost per page. In fact, using the number of clicks required as a measure, printing cost information was further away from the home page than any other information.

How can firms hide important information like printing costs, bank fees, and hotel add-ons from customers? It would seem that this is important information that buyers would like to know. If there is competition between firms selling these products, you would think that some producer would share these charges with potential buyers as a strategy to attract new customers. You would also assume that word would get around about firms that hide important information from their customers, and that as a result buyers would start to shun these producers. In either case—either through seller competition or through buyer responses—it would seem that pressures exist for consumers to get the price information they want about the product and that it cannot remain hidden for long.

So, how can information like this remain hidden? In looking at these markets in detail, Gabaix and Laibson found a distinctive structural factor in the bank services, computer printer, and hotel markets. The firms in these markets face different groups of customers, and the differences between these groups create incentives for firms to hide add-on charges. Gabaix and Laibson argued that there are two clear groups of customers in these markets. First, and most importantly, there is a group of customers that does not take these extra charges into account when buying the basic product. All that matters is the initial charge for the hotel room, the printer, or to open the bank account. They are indifferent to any add-ons and extras that may have to be paid later. The second group of customers, however, does care about these extra charges. They will ask about them, think about them, and take them into account when making their buying decisions.

Sellers can easily hide information about add-on fees and hidden charges from the first group of buyers because they don't care about the fees. Because the second group does care, you might think that their interests would dominate and that their demand for the information would eventually cause it to be openly shared. Gabaix and Laibson found, however, that in fact the second group of customers does not want this to happen. These knowledgeable buyers actually have incentives to keep the information hidden. The reason for this is that once they know the information about the add-ons and hidden fees, they can use this information to their own benefit.

The reason that a benefit exists for knowledgeable buyers is that sellers use the hidden price of add-ons as a factor in the pricing of their main product. Firms that sell computer printers, for example, sell the basic product cheaply because they make most of their money from selling replacement cartridges. In the same way, banks and hotels with add-on fees can charge a bit less for their main product in order to acquire customers who then pay the extra charges. Gabaix and Laibson found that in fact the more competitive the market, the more likely it is that the base good will have a lower price and the add-ons will be used as the source of profit. The knowledgeable buyers figure this out, of course, and understand that the hidden fees—which they can avoid to a large extent once they know about them—actually give them a better price for the initial product.

The end result is that no one cares that the fees are hidden. The first group of customers is indifferent. The firms like it because they can use add-ons as a way to charge different prices to different buyers. And the knowledgeable group of buyers knows that the hidden information actually gives them a better deal on the basic product. When these structural circumstances come together, no one has an incentive to reveal hidden fees.

You would expect that over time the group of buyers who were at first indifferent to the hidden costs will eventually find out about the hidden fees. They will, after all, have to buy new printer cartridges at some point and may well have to pay bank fees and hotel add-ons. Gabaix and Laibson found that this does occur and that as a result hidden add-ons have a life span and need to be replaced. If they are not revised or replaced, they will tend to disappear over time. Better consumer information and government regulations—such as rules requiring transparent publication of add-ons—can also cause hidden costs to be revealed. A True Fees Act has been proposed at the federal level in the United States, and the state of Massachusetts acted in 2018 to require cable TV firms to advertise accurate monthly costs. These factors act to reduce the size of the group of indifferent buyers and increase the size of the group of knowledgeable buyers. Although this can happen, Gabaix and Laibson found that two important forces keep the system going. First, new generations of indifferent buyers are always coming along. They replenish the size of the indifferent group as some of its members become more knowledgeable about the market. More importantly, the firms selling the products can act to change fee and add-on structures. If as time passes the division between the two customer groups remains strong, then the hidden fees will persist.

The best strategy as a consumer in these markets, of course, is to become a member of the group of knowledgeable buyers. If you can know about the add-on charges and fees, you can often use the information to avoid them and get a good deal on the main product being sold.

Credit Cards

As we just found, markets where firms face two distinctive groups of buyers can create the opportunity to maintain hidden fees. You will recall that a difference between distinctive groups of buyers was also important in creating the possibility for ticket scalping. In that case, the key distinction between the groups was the time when people bought their tickets, with the differences between early buyers and late buyers being a factor in creating incentives for sellers to underprice tickets for their events. In similar ways, it turns out, differences between distinctive groups of users of credit cards are important causes of high credit card rates.

The persistence of high credit card interest rates is a fact that has attracted the attention of several economists who like to puzzle over interesting prices and markets. The market actually looks like it should lead to pretty competitive results. Heaven knows, there are plenty of suppliers of credit cards. The product that is being sold is even remarkably the same across different sellers. Although fees do vary, credit card terms tend to be quite close, and card companies try to attract your attention in ways other than in the rates they charge (special gifts or rewards, special introductory terms, special card designs). In such a market, with numerous providers, apparently fairly easy entry conditions, closely similar products, and active solicitation of customers, you would expect prices to be bid down close to cost and suppliers to earn very normal profits. Yet this does not seem to happen in the credit card market. Rates seem to be remarkably sticky at levels well above those for other kinds of loans.

So, what is going on here? Several people have tried to solve this puzzle. Lawrence Ausubel, Paul Calem and Loretta Mester, and Victor Stango, among others, have looked at this result in detail. The main conclusion of these investigators is that the market for credit cards is indeed imperfect. The problem they find, however, is not on the producer side but on the consumer side of the market.

Ausubel, Calem and Mester, and Stango found that in the credit card market different buyers pay very different prices for the use of credit. At one extreme is the user of the no-annual-fee card who pays her card off on time every month, thus never paying fees or interest. These customers basically get the convenience of the credit card while paying nothing (well, there is the check, stamp, and envelope for the monthly payment—which can be avoided by online payments). At the other extreme in the spectrum of credit card users are the scammers who run up maximum bills and don't pay anything. In the middle are those who maintain a credit balance and pay regular interest to the card issuers for the privilege of carrying their loans.

Ausubel, Calam and Mester, and Stango found the fact that buyers fall into very different groups in the credit card market creates incentives that allow card issuers to keep interest rates high. In particular, they find that the customers that credit card issuers want to attract are unresponsive to lower interest rates. Since lowering interest rates does not attract the "right" customers, firms keep rates high.

The customers that card companies want to attract are people with significant card balances who make regular payments. According to the researchers looking at this market, these customers tend to be tied to their current credit card company. One factor at work is the fact that people with high levels of debt are less likely to be approved by a new card company. Another— supported by surveys of credit card users—is that people with high levels of credit card debt are less likely to change cards for small changes in the interest rates they pay. A third factor that ties people to cards is annual fees. Once people have paid these nonrefundable charges, they are reluctant to change cards and incur another fee. The end result is that the customers that credit card companies want are not very responsive to changes in the interest rates charged. A change in the rates will do little good in expanding the desired customer base. Because the most desired customers tend to be tied to their current card company, card issuers have little incentive to compete in the prices they charge, and credit card rates remain stubbornly high. The situation is quite similar to the one we found with hidden fees. The group of borrowers who do not pay any fees or interest are knowledgeable buyers. They are equivalent to the groups who know about hotel add-ons and bank fees and act to avoid the charges.

It is easy to see why credit card issuers like the group of customers who maintain balances and regularly pay their bills. But why do card issuers tolerate the customers who pay off their balances every month? Are these customers just a burden the issuer has to bear in order to get the customers they want? Actually, the answer is no. As you probably know, businesses pay a fee to card issuers every time a card is used. Card users, then, who never run a balance also generate fees for the card issuers. They just don't pay the fees themselves.

The fact that credit card issuers can get paid in each transaction from two different customers creates some interesting pricing strategies. The card issuer has to set the prices for both users, so they need to take both sides of the market into account. The price charged on one side of the market can clearly have effects that influence the other side as well. When the Federal Reserve capped debit card merchant fees in 2011, for example, card issuers raised customer fees and cut customer rewards programs. In states where it is legal, some merchants add on a surcharge to customers who use credit cards to offset the merchant fees. One interesting result of the double price market is that credit card users who pay off their balances each month can still participate in rewards programs. If a card has no annual fee and a rewards program (and you don't have to pay a surcharge), in effect these customers are actually being paid to use the card. Actually paying the customer in order to use the product makes sense because of the fees paid on the other side of the market. You have always been counseled to pay off your credit cards each month, use cards with no annual fee, and pick a card with a rewards program. Now you can see how good this advice is. Not only does following this advice save you money, but it gives you the opportunity to enjoy that rare experience as a consumer of paying a negative price, where you actually get paid to use a good.

CHAPTER SEVEN

Music and the Erie Canal, College Tuition, and Good Monopoly Prices

Technological Change, Buyer Characteristics, and Barriers to Entry as Structural Factors

We have identified a variety of structural and behavioral factors that cause the patterns we see in everyday prices and markets. Information gaps between buyers and sellers create a multitude of issues, as do differences between groups of buyers and our inherent tendencies to be overconfident, to procrastinate, and to stick with the status quo. It shouldn't surprise you to learn that this does not complete the list of factors that matter in creating market patterns. The rate and incidence of technological change is another structural feature that can have a powerful effect on market prices, as can the specific details of market structures. The particular structural circumstances in markets can come together to create challenging outcomes for both consumers and firms. The range of possibilities that structural features can create is illustrated by the impact of recent technological change on the music industry, by the factors behind the rising cost of a college education, and the possibility of "good" monopoly prices.

Music and the Erie Canal

If you have walked around a shopping mall lately, you may have noticed that the mall music store has pretty much disappeared. Every mall used to have two or more of these places. If you think about the disappearance of the mall music store for a minute, you will probably guess that buying music online has had a lot to do with it. I know I certainly enjoyed my iPod when that new technology came along. It became a near necessity when I had to take frequent plane trips. I just put on a headset and let the time flow by.

You may recall reading about the changes in the music industry that have been created by Internet technologies. There have been mergers between music labels and a lot of experimenting by musicians trying different ways to sell their work in new ways. So it seems that it is not just the mall music stores that have changed but the entire process of producing and distributing music to its fans. Why is new technology creating such a transformation in the business?

The issues that are creating change in the music business are actually quite general. If you think about it a minute, it is apparent that the product in the business is the music produced by the individual artist, and the customer is the fan who wants to own the work produced by that musician. The music labels and the music stores are intermediaries that stand between the artists and their fans. The intermediaries in the music businesses sign artists to contracts, arrange studio time to record their music, package the product, advertise it, and ship it to buyers. The music stores then buy the recorded music, display it, advertise it, and make it available in widespread locations for buyers. All these recording, packaging, shipping, advertising, and displaying services cost money. Since the product is really the music made by the artist and the listening by the fan, all of these connecting services have to be paid for out of the money that is generated by the link between the artist and their fans.

It is useful here to recall the yard sale where you got rid of your old TV. If you sold that TV for $20 to a person who was driving by, there would be no one standing between the seller and the buyer. Now imagine that there was an intermediary who took the TV off your hands and sold it for you. You probably know that there are consignment shops in your town that will do this for you. You could also sell the TV online through eBay or another auction site. What would the difference be? Clearly, the intermediary would take a part of that $20 for their services. Instead of the $20 going directly from the buyer's pocket to yours as at the yard sale, it would pass through someone else's pocket along the way, and they would take their slice. This amount will be negotiated between the seller and the intermediary. The consignment sellers I know who try to make a living at the job commonly take about a third of the total. Nonprofit consignment sellers often take less, perhaps a fourth.

If you think about it, intermediaries like this are an important part of many consumer markets. There are, of course, many cases where the connection between the producer and the buyer is direct. Everyday things that come to mind include farmers' markets, yard sales, working with your family attorney, hiring the teenager who lives next door as a babysitter, or contracting with a local lawn service. But markets with intermediaries are just as common. The whole point of department stores, hardware stores, and supermarkets is to collect products from original producers and put them in one place for your convenience. Shoe stores and clothing stores do the same thing but with a narrower focus. Your stockbroker stands between you and the investments you make in the stocks or bonds of particular issuers.

The fact that there is someone in the middle creates incentives for both the ultimate buyers and the original sellers to do something about it. If they have a choice, the buyers and sellers would rather cut out the intermediaries altogether. The intermediaries, of course, like it just the way it is, and in fact would like to improve their share if they can.

This tension between intermediaries and the buyers and sellers they serve has created some spectacular economic events. One of the most impressive in U.S. economic history was the Erie Canal. As you may remember from a past history class, the Erie is a 363-mile waterway connecting areas to the east and west of the Appalachian Mountains in the state of New York. Before the Erie Canal was built in the early 1800s, agricultural products from the Midwest mainly had to travel down the Mississippi River and up the Atlantic Coast to reach the East Coast or had to be transported across the Appalachians by horse and wagon. The tremendous intermediary transportation costs made farm prices low for Midwest farmers and high for East Coast consumers. The transport companies, of course, enjoyed the opportunities created by the process. As soon as the Erie Canal was opened, however, freight rates fell by 90 percent. As a result, the prices received by Midwest farmers went up and the prices paid by East Coast consumers went down. Together, these effects caused a surge in output. Total tonnage shipped on the canal rose thirty times over the period 1836–1860. The intermediary cost of transportation, in other words, not only reduced the well-being of both producers and consumers but it limited the growth of the market.

What the history of the Erie Canal illustrates is the ability of technological innovation to powerfully change the economic relationship between intermediaries and the buyers and sellers they stand between. In thinking about what happened to the mall music stores, it is interesting to consider that the Internet was the Erie Canal of the music business. The Internet changed the nature of the costs of connecting music artists and their fans, just like the Erie Canal reduced the costs between food producers and buyers. As a result, new forms of making those connections were created. In the music business, the first change was the rise of illegal download sites like Napster. This was followed by the rise of individual track download sites like iTunes. This in turn evolved into streaming services like Spotify. The consequences of technological changes like this for those who make a living as one of the older forms of intermediaries can be dramatic. Either their role is reduced, becomes less prosperous, becomes significantly changed, or is eliminated altogether. They fight against it, complain about it, and work to offset it, but sometimes, like the music stores in the malls, all they can do is fade away.

An interesting question is where changes like this will occur next. It is clear that book publishing is among the industries undergoing similar changes. The fundamental nature of the relation between authors and their readers is close to the connections between musicians and their listeners. Book publishers and bookstores are like music labels and music stores. They are intermediaries that stand between the artists and their fans. The question readily comes to mind that if current technologies have such a dramatic effect on the music business, do they do the same thing for books?

There are certainly differences that matter between books and music. Holding a finely crafted book in your hand and turning its pages is not the same experience as listening to a digital download or playing a vinyl recording. But the potential to change the old structures of intermediaries between the artists and their fans is similar. The number of bookstores in the United States has fallen significantly, and the mall bookstore has disappeared in the same way as the mall music store. In just one year between mid-2010 and mid-2011, the percentage of consumer electronic books sold in the United States went from one-third of the total of adult hardbacks to over one-half. Some industry watchers predict that shelf space devoted to books in physical stores will decline by 90 percent between 2010 and 2020.

The same process of innovating new ways of connecting producers to users has happened in the TV and movie businesses, where new technologies of distribution through Redbox, Netflix, tablet and smartphone applications, and new selling strategies like MoviePass have been developed. The process has also certainly been going on for some time in the airline travel industry, as online booking of flights has changed the traditional structure of the relationship between airlines and travel agents. Reducing intermediary costs is clearly what Amazon is all about, as it has expanded its offerings from selling and delivering books to what seems like almost everything else. The distress of the traditional retail intermediaries of department stores and clothes shops under the Amazon effect is clear in the lists of store closing announcements in recent years. In January 2017 alone, the list included hundreds of stores by Sears, K-Mart, Macy's, The Limited, and Wet Seal. In October 2018, Sears gave up the struggle and declared bankruptcy. As a January 2018 article on these changes put it, "A new, terrifying phrase has entered the lexicon of business jargon: being 'Amazoned.'"

Books, movies, and retail clothing clearly are not the only industries undergoing the effects of recent technological changes. In a 2018 announcement of a wholesale reorganization of its business plan, for example, a midwestern art gallery explained that "For most of our history commercial galleries were the vital link for building and maintaining relationships between artists and patrons. That has changed as technology has made our world small and direct relationships between artists and collectors have become easier and more normal." Grocery stores, toy stores, and newspapers are on the same list. The United States lost 20 percent of its newspapers between 2004 and 2018. Finding new ways to connect riders and drivers in urban areas has certainly shaken up the traditional taxi market with the rise of Uber and other ride-sharing apps. The traditional role of brokers and other intermediaries in the truck hauling business is even undergoing the same process of change with the same kinds of results. A 2016 case study of the use of new technologies connecting shippers to truckers found examples of truckers increasing their revenues by 25 percent, shippers reducing their commissions from 40 percent to 10 percent, and improved connections lowering transit times by a third. The new technologies are even affecting the market for fashion goods. The fact that new clothing designs displayed at fashion shows can be seen immediately online has caused designers to search for ways to shorten the time between shows and sales. In the fall of 2016 several designers experimented with moving the entire seasonal fashion cycle forward by several months by replacing their September spring design shows with fall designs for sale immediately. As we noted earlier, sports shoes manufacturers are developing technologies to reduce the time from design to final production from months to days.

This is a fascinating process to watch when it happens in a market. It is easy to imagine current intermediaries in the book, movie, television, clothing, and other businesses standing on a hilltop watching their own industry's Erie Canal being built before their eyes and wondering what it means for them. These can be challenging times for intermediary firms. In retail clothing, traditional brick-and-mortar stores face competition not only from pure online stores but hybrid stores like Bonobos and Paul Evans, which have clothes and shoes to try on but carry no stock so you order online what you want. The shopping mall itself is even at risk as its tenants face these challenges. Change has been particularly fast in Britain because central warehouses can deliver packages to almost all sixty-five million people living on the compact island within a day.

As a consumer, doing the best for yourself while all this is going on means having to adjust to keep up with the new ways of providing goods. This can be a challenge as it takes time to determine what is going to work best with the new technologies. In the music business, as we have found, there was a fairly rapid evolution from buying individual songs to the use of streaming services. As the experience of the Erie Canal shows, however, cutting intermediary costs can have the effect of increasing growth and lowering costs. This is certainly a boon to individual consumers. Since the new ways of selling and distributing things are spreading and developing so fast, the possible payoff in better prices and more kinds of goods and services seems to make dealing with the challenges of keeping up with the new ways of doing things well worth it to most consumers.

College Tuition

Paying for my daughters' college educations was a daunting experience. From the 1980s through 2010, the cost of attending college rose at four times the rate of inflation. The target of paying for a college education seems to be moving ever faster away, like some extreme red-shifted galaxy receding at an accelerating rate off into the universe. In fact, the thought of a red shift seems totally appropriate given the red ink implied by the deficit faced by our household budget.

An interesting set of structural and behavioral features have come together to create the issues related to college tuition. The rising cost seems puzzling at first. After all, there are literally thousands of places in the United States to get a college degree, so it seems like there should be plenty of competition in the market. There clearly is not a monopoly firm taking advantage of its position to raise prices in its favor. Certainly, buyers of college educations do not have perfect information about the product they are buying, so this is one area where the benefits of competition can break down. College is a multidimensional product, with huge variations possible in teaching quality, program content, technology availability, customer service, and the vast number of other details that matter, from parking convenience to weekend library hours. But colleges and universities spend a lot of effort trying to provide potential students with the information they need in order to decide if their institution is a good fit for them. Because college is expensive, consumers are also willing to spent lots of time collecting this information. So, although the information gap is large, there does not seem to be a problem with information asymmetry in the college market like in the markets for used cars or fashion goods.

Given the effort to provide good information and the number of places to get a college degree, you would expect there would be little opportunity for any one firm to make a great deal of money. Without some kind of collusion between sellers or some legal restriction that prevents competition, you would expect competitive results to break out in terms of output and price. In fact, this is what you do find among colleges and universities. They are not places that earn great economic profits. If you talk to people who choose careers in academia, they don't talk about salaries, bonuses, or opportunities for economic gain as reasons for their choice. If anything, they consider the financial rewards as negatives about the career path they have chosen. Great economic profits are not earned in the college education business because it is just too competitive. The fact that most colleges and universities are nonprofit organizations may change the competitive pressures a bit, but they have been this way throughout their history so this cannot be a major factor causing the recent rapid rise in college costs.

If college and university education is actually quite competitive, where does the price pressure come from? If in fact, as it seems, price increases are not being imposed by market control by the schools, then the pressures must be coming from elsewhere. Part of this may come from the government. Certainly, colleges and universities have faced new mandates in terms of the services they provide. Provision for the disabled in terms of building accessibility comes to mind, as do environmental and health requirements in dealing with such things as disposal of waste from biology and chemistry departments and the maintenance of dining facilities. Many of these requirements are new in recent years, and the institutions themselves have to provide and pay for most of them.

Although legally mandated pressures for price increases exist, the main factors at work in higher education, however, are most likely on the buyer side. As you probably know from reading news stories, studies about the value of a college education in recent years conclude that the economic importance of a college degree remains strong. The income gap between the college graduate and the high school graduate is large for both men and women. Although a significant part of this is due to falling incomes of those with just a high school degree, that does not diminish the value of earning a college degree. If you pay attention to reports on unemployment rates, you probably know as well that the unemployment rates for those with college degrees are below those with people who do not have those degrees. Part of the reason for the higher price for college education, then, is due to the fact that it is worth a lot. The fact that the percentage of people completing a college degree has risen dramatically is a clear sign that this message has gotten across to many people.

Perhaps the most important pressure on prices from the buyer side, however, is expectations about the services provided. Colleges and universities compete for students, but most importantly they are in competition for the best students. This is another example like ticket scalping, hidden fees, and credit cards where differences between groups of buyers matter for market prices. Retention and graduation rates, which are commonly used as measures of school quality, depend greatly on the background of the students who attend. In order to attract those students who can best succeed, colleges and universities need to provide what these students want.

One thing that good students want, to be sure, is a high-quality education. To provide this, institutions must have high-quality instructors in their classes and up-to-date materials and technologies. To hire the best professors and to maintain the best classroom and research facilities are expensive. Beyond the classroom, students are attracted as well by a safe environment, comfortable living spaces, high-quality medical care when needed, clean eating facilities with a wide variety of choices, entertainment options to provide release from the pressures of their studies, friendly and efficient service in taking care of administrative needs, and effective advice and assistance in making the transition to life after college. These services and amenities are costly, and colleges and universities have to provide them in order to attract and keep the students that they must have in order to survive and thrive. A recent evaluation of college tuition trends concluded that if you take all of these improvements into account, the quality-constant price of attending college may not, in fact, have increased at all.

The problem for colleges and universities in all of this is that the trends in prices over the past forty years are probably not sustainable. If something is truly nonsustainable, it will end, and when it ends, things will change. One outcome that is possible for college and university education is a different use of technology to provide their products. The process of creating reputable online classes and degree programs is well underway. Some colleges and universities are trying to reduce a college degree from a four-year to a three-year experience. Looking back to our previous discussion of mall music stores, it could well be that colleges and universities are facing their own Erie Canal moment, as technology transforms the way that their consumers get the goods that are offered.

All of this is still a way in the future, however. As I faced the challenge of paying for our daughters' college educations, it was not much consolation to reflect that the price increases creating the financial issues in higher education may well be justified by the improvements in the quality of the experience that is being provided. There was also not much solace in thinking that these changes are probably my own fault. I know I certainly had high expectations for our daughters' four-year experience in terms of teaching, advising, safety, comfort, availability of choice, counseling, and all of the other dimensions that I hoped would create an engaging and productive transition to adulthood. I was aware that the competitive pressure college and universities face to attract good students by providing these high-quality amenities comes at a high cost and thus a high price. Even though I knew all this, there was not much I could do other than encourage my daughters to look more broadly at the options for colleges to attend, apply for available scholarships, and resolve to add more each month to their college fund.

Good Monopoly Prices

Want to hook up to natural gas, or arrange for garbage collection, or get delivery of domestic water? As you well know, you only have the choice of one provider of these goods in your area (almost always—there actually are places with more than one seller of these services). And as you are also probably quite aware, in most cases the prices these sellers charge for their services are controlled by some government agency. The reason for this regulation is that everyone expects that sole sellers of desirable products will take advantage of their privileged position if they are left alone and will set quite high prices for their products.

This is all very true and commonly the case with monopoly goods. Certainly, companies like Apple and Microsoft have done very well for themselves with the legal monopolies they have acquired by inventing and patenting goods that people want to buy. In the late 2010s, a major policy concern developed over whether the U.S. economy was becoming less competitive as monopolies and other firms with market power became more aggressive in expanding and entrenching their market controls. A 2016 study found that nearly two-thirds of American industries had become more concentrated in the 2000s.

Interestingly, however, there are also several plausible cases in which monopoly prices may be quite reasonable. How profitable, for example, do you think the last maker of buggy-whips will be? The only reason they still exist is that every other firm has been driven out of the market by falling sales and prices. The last firm hangs on because they are just efficient enough to survive at the lower prices and there is just enough demand for the product to keep them going. The idea of a last surviving firm may seem unusual, but there are probably more of these kinds of "monopolies" around than you think. It is just that no one pays much attention to the last producer of slide rules or the last home-delivery service for dairy products in a community.

To see another type of monopoly that will actually charge reasonable prices, imagine that you are living in Outback, Nevada, and need to fly to Chicago. Your only choice at the Outback Community Airport is to buy a ticket at the Quick-and-Comfy Airlines counter because they fly the only planes in town. Now suppose that Quick-and-Comfy decides to take advantage of its monopoly position at Outback and doubles its fares. What may well happen quite quickly? With good money being made on the Outback route, it would be attractive to other firms. It is likely that some other airline would arrange to fly into town, and there would soon be competitive pressure on prices.

Does this happen? Yes, it does, and airlines are an example of an industry where the existence of potential entrants waiting to jump in at opportunities where a profit is being made can serve to limit monopoly price levels. As a result, even routes flown by only one or two airlines can have quite competitive rates.

This price-limiting effect is not perfect; what makes it work is the knowledge that other firms actually can start flying high-fare routes quite easily. If the Outback Community Airport is so small that there is room for only one ticket counter and one landing gate, then the Quick-and-Comfy Airlines won't worry about potential entrants. To make the price-limiting effect of possible competition work, there must be low entry barriers facing new firms.

A study of how airlines reacted to potential entry by Southwest Airlines found exactly these effects. Austan Goolsbee and Chad Syverson looked at situations where Southwest operated flights out of two airports but did not fly between those airports. In these cases, the barriers to entry were low since Southwest already was operating at both ends of the flight. Using historical data, Goolsbee and Syverson were able to calculate that the probability that Southwest would start flying between the two airports was 18.5 percent in the current quarter of the year if they had flights out of both of the endpoints in the previous quarter. Potential entry in these cases, then, was a real threat, and the authors found that the airlines already operating flights between the two airports reacted accordingly. The current airlines lowered their fares significantly in response to the threat and increased the number of passengers they carried. There was no evidence that these fare cuts were due to decreased costs, and the airlines did not extend them to other routes where Southwest was not a direct threat. Goolsbee and Syverson interpreted these fare cuts as attempts to deter Southwest from entering the route. As their data showed, it seems quite clear that when barriers are low and potential entry quite feasible that existing airlines will react by charging very competitive fares.

Another case where a monopoly may charge quite reasonable prices can be seen by extending the Quick-and-Comfy Airlines example. Assume that a train serves the same route as the airline. For many products, cases exist like this where different goods are seen by consumers as fulfilling almost the same need. If people see taking the train and taking the plane as nearly the same thing, then Quick-and-Comfy will have to charge reasonable prices even if direct entry into the airline market is not possible. Closely comparable products serve the same role as direct competition. There are many situations like this. Having a monopoly in the production of aluminum doesn't do you much good if copper or steel can easily be substituted by buyers. Having control of overland telephone lines is not worth much if other firms can transmit the same calls by Internet or satellite.

So far, we have found that our hypothetical monopoly Quick-and-Comfy Airlines will charge reasonable prices if they are the last firm in a disappearing market or if they face the possibility of easy entry by a direct competitor. We also found that even if direct entry is not possible reasonable prices may exist if there is a closely comparable service available. One other possibility that can create reasonable prices in a monopoly market is the length of time a monopoly can expect to keep competitors out of its market.

If Quick-and-Comfy's market is well protected and the firm decides to charge high prices, it probably can have the market to itself for a period of time. But if the airline is making high profits, then eventually someone will try to get around the barriers. To stop this potential entry, Quick-and-Comfy may decide not to create too tempting a target. One way to do this is to keep their prices at a more reasonable level.

If Quick-and-Comfy keeps their prices reasonable, they can discourage other firms from making investments in competing products and may keep the market to themselves for a long time. The choice Quick-and-Comfy faces is either to make as much money as they can in the short run and lose their monopoly in a fairly short time, or to take reasonable profits that can continue for the long term. The issue comes down to which is most profitable in the long run. Under many reasonable assumptions, the best choice will be to charge reasonable prices now in order to preserve market control over time.

Two contrasting examples from the early twentieth century show the choices that can be made. After it was formed in the early 1900s, U.S. Steel had a near monopoly position in the steel market. The company decided to set high prices and take maximum profits in the short run. As a consequence, U.S. Steel saw its market share steadily erode as new firms entered the market. Alcoa, which was formed near the same time, had a similar monopoly position in the production of aluminum. In contrast to U.S. Steel, however, Alcoa kept prices reasonable, took a long flow of regular profits, and maintained its market share for years at a steady level (until government actions disrupted the market during and after World War II).

Of course, a monopolist may well choose to take advantage of its privileged market position and charge high prices for its products. The key structural factor causing even monopolies and near monopolies to charge "good" prices is facing a situation where the entry of direct competitors is a real possibility. The encouraging news for consumers is that this incentive for competitors to come up with ways to take away markets from monopolies is a strong one. Although Polaroid, U.S. Steel, and the original AT&T made fortunes for their founders, their monopolies did not last. All three had their market positions eroded by the entry of new firms with competing products. The leaders of current firms know this history well. When asked in an interview in November 2018 what he thought would happen in the long run to Amazon, Jeff Bezos, who founded the company, said: "I predict one day Amazon will fail. Amazon will go bankrupt."

This process, however, is not automatic. Amazon, Spotify, and the other new technology firms that are building modern versions of the Erie Canal to connect producers and consumers will do all they can to protect and defend the markets they have created for themselves. A common strategy for successful firms is to try to build on the success in their initial market and find new products and services to provide. At their beginnings, Apple just produced computers, Amazon only sold books, and Microsoft produced operating systems for personal computers. The ability to extend success in an initial market is not guaranteed, however. Intel failed in its attempt to produce digital cameras, AT&T had no success when it entered the credit card business, and Microsoft spent billions but failed in selling phones. The ultimate message for consumers is that competition can break out in even highly concentrated markets, with beneficial results in terms of product variety and price.

What happens over time depends in large part on policy. For competitive effects to occur, policy makers must create and maintain a legal environment that does not allow firms with market power to eliminate competition. As evidence accumulated in the late 2010s that market concentration had increased in American industries and that current policy responses were inadequate, the focus centered on policies to reduce barriers to entry in existing markets. Whether Jeff Bezos is right in his prediction for the future of Amazon may depend on the outcome of these discussions.

CHAPTER EIGHT

Shopping Malls, Whales, and Prescription Drugs

The Absence of Normally Expected Features in Markets

The structural and behavioral factors we have looked at so far—from technological change to information gaps to the tendency of people to discount the future—affect prices and price patterns when they are an important presence in a market. It turns out that pricing patterns can also be influenced when something we normally expect to see in a market is missing. The absence of structural features normally found in markets explains much, for example, about why big reputable stores moved to shopping malls from downtown shopping districts, why many animals face extinction, and why we pay the prices we do for prescription drugs.

Shopping Malls

Many of us may actually enjoy a trip to the mall. Next time you take a break in the food court to enjoy a fresh pretzel (extra salt) and a large soda (diet, but lots of caffeine), consider the question of why the mall even exists in the first place. Sure, there is convenient parking, comfortable climate control, and bright colorful displays. And sure, your friends hang out there and the food court choices are great. But you probably know that some malls fail and that before malls existed central city shopping districts provided the same services and stores. A little reflection suggests that the essence of what works for malls seems to be the bunching of shopping places in the same location. Why does this matter? What is going on here?

Your feeling that the bunching of stores at the mall must be important is right on the money. It simply makes sense that shoppers are attracted to collections of stores. If you like to visit antique stores, where will you most likely choose to shop? Will you go to a place with a dozen great antique stores within walking distance, or to an isolated single store? Many people will pick the collection of shopping choices. For the same reason, if you want to shop for upscale goods when you visit Los Angeles, Rodeo Drive in Beverly Hills is the place to go.

It is just as clear, though, that not all collections of stores are equal. What makes you willing to drive an hour to that great mall in the next town compared to that not-so-great mall 20 minutes away? Is it the mall electronics store? The shoe store? The jewelers? Most likely not. The key to a successful mall seems to be the good anchor store—and the more good ones the better. A mall with Nordstrom, Neiman-Marcus, Apple, and Macy's seems a better place than one anchored by The Save-a-Lot Co. and Only Cheap Goods Inc.

The importance to the success of a shopping area of an anchor store with a big reputation has been clear for decades. When a developer starts a mall project, the first thing she does is sign up the anchor stores. Everything else follows. The importance of an anchor store with a strong reputation was true even in premall days. If you look at past successful central city shopping districts, you will almost always find they had at their core a reputable big store that brought the people in.

Because the attractive big store has positive implications for shoppers, it has the same attraction for smaller stores. Say you are a small specialty dress-shop owner. Where would you want to locate, in the regional supermall between Nordstrom and Macy's, or in the local strip mall between Pat's Haircuts (Walk-ins Welcome!) and J.J.'s Liquor (Special on Local Brews!)? As the anchor stores pull in the customers, small stores located nearby benefit. As a result, successful anchor stores create successful malls full of thriving smaller stores. And, of course, the process works in reverse as well. Malls that lose major anchors tend to lose their high-quality small stores soon after, to be replaced by empty spaces and discount shops.

There is a concept here that has wide applicability beyond the creation of malls. The anchor stores create side effects that are called "positive externalities." People tend to be willing to travel a fair distance to the "good" mall because of the "good" anchor stores. The shoppers they attract are a positive externality to small specialty stores that is created by the presence of the successful big store. This worked in older downtown shopping districts just as it does in malls.

Externalities—both positive and negative—are quite common. You actually know a lot about them from everyday life. The noise from your neighbor's dog—the one that barks right outside your bedroom window when your neighbor is not at home—is a negative externality. The noisy airplane flying overhead, the large tree next door that blocks your view of the river, the guy that sits next to you in math class and taps his pencil all the time are all negative externalities for you. Some goods or actions would not seem to have externalities, such as your friend eating a hamburger. But externalities can exist here, too. Now that she has had lunch she may be less irritable—a positive externality for you. But on the other hand if she had double onions on the burger, and you have to sit close and talk to her on the bus home, there could be a negative externality for you.

The essence of markets that have externalities is that important benefits or costs associated with a good are not reflected in the price charged to consumers. Instead these benefits and costs get passed along to others. In effect, externalities constitute a breakdown in the ideal functioning of markets. The result, when negative externalities exist, is that the market price is too low and too much of the good is produced because costs to others are not accounted for in the market price. When positive externalities exist, the market price is too high and too little of the good is produced because the benefits from the good to others are not accounted for by the individuals who buy the good.

An excellent example of a negative externality is air or water pollution. Pollution is essentially free garbage disposal. Instead of paying to have the waste they generate during production disposed of properly, polluters get rid of it for free by dumping it into the air or water. As a result of this free garbage disposal, the price of the good does not reflect all of the costs of its production. Other people, of course, then pay these costs by having to live with the effects of the pollution or paying to have it removed. This is the foundation of the argument for a carbon tax, which would raise the price of products with high carbon emissions to account for the negative externality of their contribution to global warming.

Another example of a negative externality appears to occur in the side effects created by ride-hailing firms like Uber and Lyft. Bruce Schaller has found that ride hailing seems to increase congestion in cities, by his calculations adding 2.8 miles of driving in cities for every mile that the service subtracts. John Barrios, Yael Hochberg, and Hanyi Yi found in another study that in addition to increasing vehicle miles driven, gasoline consumption, and car registrations, ride hailing leads to a 3.5 percent rise in fatal car accidents, amounting to 987 extra deaths per year in the United States.

On the other hand, education provides an excellent example of a positive externality. Education, of course, benefits the person who receives it. But your education also has positive effects for others around you. Educated people tend to be more responsible citizens, better employees, and have a wider breadth and depth of interests that they share with others. Since the people who buy education for themselves do not get these extra benefits, they do not include them in their decisions about how much education to receive.

A standard recommendation to solve externality problems is government intervention, such as the carbon tax, auto industry requirements to reduce air pollution, or the provision of free public education. It doesn't have to be this way, however. If the number of people involved is not large, there are clear property rights, and it is not costly for the people involved to communicate with each other, externalities may be resolved by private agreements. A case arose not long ago in Washington State involving property owners around a Cascade Mountains' lake and the lumber company that owned a large mountain overlooking the lake. When the lumber company announced plans to log the trees from the side of the mountain facing the lake, the lakeside owners—concerned about the negative externality of the loss of a spectacular view from their homes and damage to the watershed—banded together and made an offer to buy the mountain from the lumber company. In this case, the number of people bearing the cost of the negative externality was only a few dozen; they already had a long-standing community association to improve the quality of the lake and its surroundings; and the property rights of the logging company to the land on the mountain were clear. The result was a voluntary settlement that compensated the logging company for the loss of income from logging and preserved the view and lake quality for the lakeside owners. ·

Although negative externalities like pollution tend to get most of the publicity, positive externalities like those that create shopping malls are just as common. Vaccinations, for example, are another clear case. You are willing to pay to get a flu shot because it will prevent you from becoming ill. But your act also benefits others. If you can't get sick, then you can't give the flu to others, so those around you will realize positive benefits as well. Because of the importance of widespread health benefits to others from vaccinations, a common solution is government intervention, including mandates for children to receive inoculations and subsidies to reduce the cost of flu shots.

It is clear that popular anchor stores create positive externalities for small shops in their neighborhoods the same way as flu shots. They act like a magnet that attracts customers, who can often be tempted by small stores to drop in as they walk by. So, given that reputable anchor stores seem to generate external benefits, why did they leave the older shopping districts for the malls? A lot of factors were at work behind this change, including expanded car ownership, improved roads, and people moving from cities to the suburbs. But perhaps there has also been a more basic financial motive at work.

In an article on this topic, B. Peter Pashigian and Eric Gould argued that in the old shopping districts anchor stores received little or no compensation for the external benefits they created, but in the new malls they did. Pashigian and Gould found that anchor stores at malls pay rents that are far below those paid by other mall stores (over 70 percent less in their sample). In effect, the big attractive stores received a subsidy from mall developers because of the positive externalities they created, and the small speciality stores paid a premium for the same reason. Pashigian and Gould even found that department stores in super-regional malls paid lower rents than those in smaller regional malls, presumably because of the greater externalities they generated. Pashigian and Gould suggested that this difference in compensation may have been why so many large stores moved out of central business districts. Their policy recommendation was that cities with older downtown areas learn the "lessons of the mall" and allow developers to control multiblock areas so they can charge rental prices that take account of the externalities between stores.

As the examples of malls, vaccinations, and pollution suggest, externalities are a common feature of everyday markets. National parks belong here, as do public libraries, municipal museums, support for the arts, national defense, and financial institutions that are judged too big to fail. The result when externalities exist is a mix of goods in the marketplace that does not ideally reflect all the costs and benefits associated with production and consumption of those goods. As noted before, the common consequence is a call for some kind of government policy to take into account the externalities missed in the market price. Because of government intervention in these markets, as a consumer you get to enjoy the benefits of lower prices created by subsidies to libraries, education, parks, and concerts, but in turn have to pay higher prices for the costs imposed by pollution controls, auto gas mileage rules, and financial regulations.

Since these are political decisions, you have the opportunity to express your opinion about all these policies and programs through candidates you support when you vote. As you do so, it is valuable to keep in mind that the economic goal of these programs is to account for real benefits and real costs that are missed and not accounted for in the market prices you pay. If you don't vote to force some externalities to be considered, markets alone will not create ideal results.

Whales

Whales provide an example of what can happen if another normally expected feature is missing in markets. Many species of whales are at risk of extinction. Humpback and fin whales were declared endangered species in the 1950s. Eight more whale species were added to the U.S. endangered list in the 1970s. Attempts were made to declare and enforce a worldwide moratorium on all whaling in the 1980s. Whales, of course, are not alone in facing possible extinction. The fate of large animals—elephants, tigers, grizzly bears, condors—gets most of the attention, but the roll of species in jeopardy ranges far into the lists of insects, plants, birds, and other living things.

Despite the attention given to endangered species, it is quite apparent that many animals are in no danger of going the way of the dodo, the passenger pigeon, or the blaauwbock. Other kinds of animals seem to be doing quite well. Horses, dogs, cats, chickens, cows, sheep, and goats would seem to be secure forever as vibrant species. What is the difference between these prospering animals and those that are endangered? Is it their size or the places where they live?

There is actually an important economic factor that matters here. The major economic difference between chickens and condors is that someone owns the chickens and no one owns the condors. The issue comes down to property rights. Clear ownership rights are one of the basic features of most markets. When such rights are missing, markets can break down and a variety of less than ideal results can follow.

The problem that is created by unclear or missing property rights is that these rules matter very much in terms of how people act toward resources. Whales and other endangered species provide a good example, but the issue is a more general one. The problem in its broadest application is called "the tragedy of the commons." When any resource is owned "in common" and not specifically by any one person or institution, then the incentives are for everyone to exploit the resource but for no one to take care of it.

Whales are a classic example of a "common" good. There are many useful products that can be derived from whales: oil, ivory, ambergris, baleen, and meat. As a result, there are good reasons to hunt and kill them. But the herds of whales that range freely across the world's oceans are not owned by anyone and thus are not carefully maintained like herds of cows and flocks of chickens. Elephants, tigers, and condors are obvious similar cases. But so are overgrazing on the Great Plains of the United States, the collapse of world fisheries of all kinds, and the pollution of air and water.

If the lack of property rights can create the wastage of a common good, can the creation of adequate property rights help stop the destruction? The answer is yes, but the process of creating enforceable property rights is a difficult one. The record of elephant herds in the south of Africa during the 1980s implied an optimistic answer. Elephant populations grew significantly in the region after the countries of southern Africa created a system of exclusive, transferable, hunting licenses. The licenses were awarded to villages or parks, which in turn sold them to hunters. Those villages and parks that increased the size of herds in their area got more licenses. As a result of setting up this system of property rights in elephants, villagers had incentives to protect herds from poachers and to take efforts to increase their size. The same practices have been tried with a variety of the world's fisheries with success in cases where the rights could be clearly awarded and monitored. But this success is difficult to maintain. Due to poaching, the total elephant population in Africa fell by one-third between 2007 and 2014.

Another kind of solution to the waste of a common good is provided by the history of cattlemen's associations in the western United States. The range land that cattlemen used was federal land. Without exclusive property rights, the result was that many areas quickly became overgrazed. A response to the problem was the formation of cattlemen's associations. As described by Timothy Tregarthen, these associations attempted to come up with methods to limit grazing on public land. An effective solution developed in Montana was that associations refused to allow nonmembers to participate in joint roundups and in the use of jointly owned corrals. This exclusion raised the production costs of nonmembers enough to keep them off the ranges in the associations' regions and thus allowed the associations to control the level of grazing in their areas even though they did not own the land.

An effective solution, of course, is to create complete ownership rights in the resource. The buffalo continues to survive in the United States because most herds are privately owned today. No one had an incentive to protect the massive herds that roamed the Great Plains. Today, however, when you can charge for people to come on your land and view a small herd grazing on that back 100 acres where nothing but scrub grows, the future of the buffalo is more assured.

If complete or a form of partial ownership is not possible, then the protection of common resources depends on the good will and good sense of people in general. About all that can be done in those cases is call for action and attempt to raise levels of consciousness about the issues involved. So those who care about saving the whales (or elephants, or tigers, or condors) do everything from taking to the streets to taking to the Internet and lobbying their local politicians to get their message across.

Prescription Drugs

A patented prescription drug is the same if you buy it by mail, through the Internet, or at your corner pharmacy. Since you know that the product is identical everywhere, shouldn't the price be the same at every location?

From our earlier candy bar story we already know that it is in fact quite likely that the price of the drug may vary from place to place. When you pick up a prescription, it costs you more than just the price of the drug. It may take you 20 minutes to pick it up at the small local pharmacy, an hour at the big discount place across town, and three days by mail. If you are busy and have procrastinated until you are down to your last pill, or you are feeling ill and need that prescription right now, it makes a lot of sense to pay a little more and get the drug at your local pharmacy rather than invest time and energy in finding a better price.

It is very understandable, then, that identical prescription drugs may not have identical prices because of the time involved in buying them. In a relevant article, Alan Sorensen looked into the range of prescription drug prices that actually exists in markets to see the magnitude of these effects. Using two small towns in New York as a sample, he collected detailed price information on a wide range of prescription drugs in about two dozen pharmacies. The pattern of prices Sorensen found fit very well with the argument that the time involved in searching for prices was a key factor in drug price variation. One of Sorensen's hypotheses was that one-time drug purchases would have a wider price range than prices for drugs that people bought regularly. It wouldn't be worth the time to shop widely for a one-time purchase, but it would be worth looking around for a drug you had to buy every month for the foreseeable future. In his sample, Sorensen found exactly this pattern with one-time prescriptions having a price range that was 34 percent larger than that of prescriptions that were bought monthly.

Given that prescription drugs are identical between stores, what would you expect the highest price to be compared to the lowest price in a small town of ten pharmacies? Strikingly, Sorensen found that the average difference was over 50 percent in his sample. Now of course, as you well know, not all pharmacies are alike. Some are friendly, comfortable, and quick to fill a prescription. Others are impersonal, sterile, and keep you waiting 30 minutes even if no one else is in line. Sorensen attempted to take these differences into account but could only attribute one-third of the price differences he found to these service-quality factors.

One factor at work affecting this result is insurance. Many people have set copayments for prescriptions. The pharmacy price means nothing to them because they don't pay it. If a significant number of buyers do not care much about the market price, it is likely that this would work as well to create a wide range of prices for identical drugs. That prescription drug prices can vary widely even with insurance was shown in a 2018 article by Lisa Gill that focused on Medicare beneficiaries. Comparing the prices for five generic drugs for three Medicare Part D plans between two pharmacies in six cities, Gill found that annual cost differences varied between 68 and 367 percent. By shifting between pharmacies and plans in the city with the smallest differences, consumers could save over $300 per year.

Interestingly, E. Woodrow Eckard was able to extend Alan Sorenson's study of price ranges for identical goods using a 1901 survey of prices for four different products from over 1,500 stores across the United States. Remarkably, three of the four products were still sold a hundred years later (baking powder, granulated sugar, and kerosene), so Eckard could do his own survey to compare to the one in 1901. Given the changes in communication and transportation over a hundred years, you might think that the dispersion of prices would have been greater in 1901 than in 2001. After all, with print ads delivered to your door every day, TV advertising, the Internet, and telephones and cars dramatically more common, it would seem that the costs of collecting information about prices would have fallen significantly. Contrary to these expectations, however, Eckard found that the dispersion of prices for all three of the products in 2001 was not lower, and in fact may have been somewhat higher. Eckard's explanation for this result was similar to Sorenson's: the economic value of time. Eckard found that sugar, baking powder, and kerosene were much more expensive relative to consumer incomes in 1901 compared to 2001, so by 2001 it was not worth spending much time looking for better prices for these goods. The improvements in information and transportation apparently closely offset the increasing costs of spending time collecting the information, so the dispersion of local prices for his three products remained approximately the same.

Sorenson's study of local drug prices in the late 1990s found that you could save over $10 on over half of the prescriptions in his sample if you bought at the lowest- compared to the highest-priced local pharmacy. It turns out that there was another key factor at work creating the large price dispersions in this market. This is a feature that is missing in the prescription drug market that you find in almost all other consumer markets. To see this factor at work, take a look at the drugstore ads the next time you get those weekly flyers in the mail. How many of the ads give you the prices of the prescriptions the pharmacy offers? Most likely that number is zero. Advertising of prescription prices is controlled in most places in the United States and was in the towns that Sorensen sampled. One of the fundamental roles of advertising is to tell buyers where products are sold and their prices. If advertising is restricted, then markets will not work as well for consumers because the search costs to find relevant prices will be higher. As a result, you would expect the range of prices charged by sellers of identical products to be larger when advertising is prohibited.

What is the message for you the next time you need to buy a prescription? If you have to pay for the drug yourself and if you have the time (and that "if" is important, as you know), it may well pay you to make some phone calls and do some Internet searches before you buy. When a normal information practice like advertising is missing, the range of prices for even very similar goods can be surprisingly large even in a small geographic area.

As the examples of shopping malls, whales, and prescription drugs show, the patterns we come across in everyday markets and prices can clearly be affected when a structural feature we normally expect to find is missing in a market. The fact that firms do not have to pay for the disposal of toxins in the air and water is a major cause of pollution. The lack of property rights is a central factor behind the near extinction of many plant and animal species. The absence of advertising can create a large range of prices for even identical goods in a small geographic area. Understanding the reasons for the pricing patterns we see in these markets can lead to a better appreciation of the efforts made by people to correct the problems that these missing structural factors create. When externalities exist, these often involve legislation. In the case of endangered species or other common goods, they often involve voluntary attempts to create cooperative action among groups or campaigns to raise public awareness. In cases where the prices of goods are not readily available, such as when advertising is prohibited, these efforts involve individual decisions to find better information before acting. In each case, these are perfectly sensible strategies to make everyday markets and prices work better for their users.

CHAPTER NINE

Halloween Candy, Soft Drinks, Senior Citizen Discounts, and College Grants

Buying More at a Lower Price as a Behavioral Factor

Markets that are missing normally expected features like property rights and advertising, that are undergoing rapid technological change, or that have significant information gaps between buyers and sellers can be challenging for consumers to deal with. Fortunately, not every market has these structural characteristics, so you don't have to worry about them every time you go shopping.

There is a feature that exists in almost every market, however, that does present daily challenges. That factor is the behavioral tendency for people to buy more of a good at a lower price. Earlier I commented that it is only in recent years that the variety of behaviors that affect economic decisions has been a topic of special study. That doesn't mean that economists have not been aware of these biases for a long time. John Maynard Keynes, for example, in his 1936 book that created the framework for modern mainstream macroeconomics, argued that people and firms are motivated by the "spontaneous optimism" of "animal spirits." In Keynes's argument, "animal spirits" create a bias toward overconfidence, as "the thought of ultimate loss . . . is put aside as a healthy man puts aside expectation of death." The result, to Keynes, was that "slumps and depressions are exaggerated in degree."

The behavioral tendency of people to buy more of a good at a lower price has an even more venerable background among economists. Alfred Marshall in his 1890 book that created the framework for modern microeconomics argued that this tendency was the central factor behind the demand side of markets. This demand behavior became seen as so deeply embedded a pattern in markets that it became one of the few generalizations that is called a "law" in economics. The reason for this behavioral tendency is clear. Most of us only have a limited amount of income to spend, and lower prices clearly make that money go farther. Because we are so used to dealing with this bias, we get pretty good at coping with price patterns based on it. There are, however, practices that we should be aware of where firms can try to use this tendency to their own advantage.

Halloween Candy

You know from past experience that the price of Halloween candy falls dramatically right after October 31. The cut is often 50 percent, and you have even seen reductions of 75 percent or more. You see the same thing happen with Christmas wrapping paper, Easter candy, and Fourth of July decorations. The reason, of course, is obvious. The holiday is over and people don't need that stuff anymore, at least for another year. The seller can store the things away, of course, but that costs money. Halloween candies and Valentine's chocolates are perishable, so storage is not even an option for goods like these. So the sellers cut the prices of these goods to get rid of them.

There are actually two things going on with the demand changes that cause these price cuts. The first, clearly, is that people need the goods before the holiday and they don't need them afterward. This fall in demand is quick and large. But not only does the demand fall, it also changes in another important way. Before the holiday people are less sensitive to the prices charged for holiday goods than they are afterward. Before the holiday they will buy more at a lower price and shy away from high prices, as we all do all the time. But before the holiday people are inclined to be less put off by higher prices. When you run out of Christmas wrapping paper on December 23 and hurry off to the store to buy some more, you may not even look at the price. When you finally get around to buying that box of Valentine's chocolates at 8:00 p.m. on February 13, you buy whatever they have and don't worry about what it costs.

Right after the holidays, that insensitivity to price changes along with the strength of demand. Once the big day has passed, you are not even tempted by high prices that existed just 24 hours ago. Sellers are going to have to do a lot to catch your attention to get you to consider buying anything at all. As a result, not only do the prices fall for leftover holiday items, they have to fall a lot to get rid of the goods.

The nature of these shifts explains why the price of seasonal goods and goods for celebrations like birthday wrapping paper have different pricing patterns than holiday goods. Birthdays, after all, happen every day, so there is no dramatic before-and-after change like with Halloween or Valentine's Day.

Demand for seasonal goods like patio furniture, garden hoses, and grass seed certainly changes as the season ends, but the transitions here are not as sudden as for holidays, and the change in price sensitivity is not as large. As a result, the price declines to clear the stock of seasonal goods are more spread out over time and are less extreme.

If you are aware of these price patterns and the reasons for them, you can use them to your advantage. It makes good sense to stock up on holiday wrapping paper in the 75 percent off racks, to pay attention to the price declines in seasonal merchandise if you need to replace that patio table umbrella, and to plan ahead so you do not have to buy holiday goods at the last minute when you may be tempted to buy something no matter how high the price.

Soft Drinks

It is the behavioral tendency to buy more if the price is lowered that explains the prices that you typically see when you look at a restaurant menu and see the charges for small, medium, and large soft drinks. As you have noticed, a common practice is to charge a fairly large amount per ounce for the small size but to charge a lower amount per ounce for the medium and large sizes. This pattern also shows up on the menu in the price of milkshakes and french fries. You see the same thing in clothing stores when they have "buy one and get the second 50 percent off" sales for shirts and socks.

There are, of course, exceptions to this "law of demand." Snob appeal goods—goods you buy more for display than for use—try to attract you with higher rather than lower prices. If you require a specific medication to stay alive, you will pay any price for the quantity you need. You will never buy some goods, say cigarettes or alcohol, no matter how low their prices. And restaurants can give free refills on soft drinks or sell all sizes of french fries at the same price as incentives to get you to stop in and buy other meals.

The behavioral decision-making process of being willing to buy more of a good at a lower price is so common, however, that it explains all kinds of price patterns. This feature of our demand for goods, for example, explains the pricing of the fancy new gizmos at your local consumer electronics store. Just as you know from past experience that the price of Halloween candy falls dramatically the day after you pack your party costume away in the closet, you know that new consumer electronic devices tend to start out at high prices that fall over time. In recent years you have seen this happen to DVDs, HD TVs, computer tablets, and smartphones. You may have kept track of these changes when you followed the falling prices of HD TVs until they got to a level where you were willing to buy. If you have been around long enough, you may remember the same thing happening to personal cassette recorders, VHS players, and CDs. The sellers of all of these new products have tight control of their brands and prices when the goods are introduced. So, why do they price these delightful new things in this way? They obviously could just price low and sell a lot to everyone from the very start. The reason they start high and lower the price over time, of course, is that the sellers of consumer technology know that there are a good number of people who really want to have that coming new thing. Since the size of this group is significant, they have found that the most profitable strategy is to start the price high and sell to this group first. As time goes by, the producers then lower the price and sell to the rest of us.

It is the sensitivity of buyers to different prices that causes consumer technology producers to start selling new products at high prices and then lower them over time. If the demand for a new good has different sensitivity characteristics, this introductory pricing strategy will differ. In fact, if demand characteristics are of a special kind, then an incentive exists for firms to do exactly the opposite of consumer technology producers. In these markets, firms begin at the other end of the demand curve, start with very low prices, and move to higher prices over time. For some goods the best strategy for sellers of a new product is even to start out by pricing their goods at zero and giving their product away.

Now this seems like a very strange decision indeed. A zero price seems like a guarantee of disaster for a firm entering a new market. If the demand for a product has the right features, however, the strategy is worth trying. A key feature that characterizes products that start with a zero price is that the demand of an individual for the product depends almost completely on how many other people are using it. Since an individual is only willing to use the product if everyone they know is using it, the seller must get the product into the hands of a large number of people very quickly. Giving a good away is just about the best possible way to do this. A second important feature in these markets is that once people start using the product they are unlikely to change to using something similar. The best examples in recent times are social network websites like Facebook and Twitter. It doesn't cost you any money as a new customer to set up your personal account and get started. The attraction to you, of course, is that everyone you know is doing the same thing, so you can connect with them all. Once you and your friends are all there together, however, it is difficult for everyone to move over to a different provider of the same service.

The challenge for the providers of these goods is, of course, to figure out how to make money once they have signed everyone up. Google is the model here. Google figured out the money-making part very well through selling advertising opportunities to firms attracted by the number of Google users and became incredibly successful. Once fees are being charged, the success of the zero introductory price strategy will depend on how strongly users are locked in to using the product. If the users stay around, then the strategy works. If they leave, however, then you have what happened as Myspace was replaced by Facebook. Facebook and Twitter provided interesting examples of this process because they started at about the same time and used the same zero-price moving to positive-price strategy. In its early years Facebook had good success in keeping and building customers as it figured out how to make money from the service it provides, but Twitter struggled to make the same transition. With Google as a model, it is easy to see why firms are willing to take the gamble and see if the strategy works for what they have to sell.

A different example of firms responding to your bias to buy more at a lower price and less at a higher price is Uber's use of "surge pricing" for taxi rides or your local freeway's use of variable tolls. These are examples of prices that vary frequently in an attempt to adjust for changes in demand. Freeway tolls are higher during periods of peak traffic to reduce the number of cars. Uber fares rise during periods of peak demand to reduce the number of riders and to draw more drivers into the market. The same type of pricing strategy is used by some electric utilities to encourage people to move their electric use for appliances like dishwashers and dryers to lower price off-peak hours.

As a consumer you need to be aware that firms can try to take advantage of this behavioral bias. When that restaurant tempts you to buy a large size soft drink by lowering the price to buy more ounces or that clothing store to buy one and get the second at half price, your best strategy is to remember what you are really trying to do with your income. As you spread your income across the variety of goods you buy, your goal should be to maximize the satisfaction you get from your total spending. The restaurant and the clothing store are trying to get you to do something different. By lowering the price for added ounces or for a second shirt the restaurant and the clothing store are encouraging you to maximize the number of ounces or shirts you can get per dollar. They are attempting to take advantage of your behavioral biases to buy more at a lower price by offering a tempting deal to make you forget for a minute your real goal in spending your money. The story that comes to mind whenever I face this choice was told to me by my friend Chuck who says that he regularly bought a large size drink at his favorite place to eat because of the low price for the extra amount. Chuck eventually realized, however, that the extra amount he drank made him feel queasy and uncomfortable and not enjoy the rest of his meal. When he figured that out, he switched to the smaller size, better enjoyed his meal, saved a little money, and got more satisfaction out of his trips to the restaurant.

A good strategy when firms tempt you to forget what you are really trying to maximize when you spend your money is to remember Chuck's story. The hesitation may be just enough to make you walk away from the deal. When you are faced with firms offering a snazzy new electronic product at a high price, the best strategy is to be patient and watch what happens over time. The price will often fall fairly quickly, especially if other firms enter the market with something similar to offer. If you are faced with firms trying to draw you in as a customer by giving their product away, then you should be aware that they will try to lock you in and charge positive prices in the future. In particular, you should be aware that even though you may continue to pay a zero dollar fee for an online service you are actually paying a positive price with your personal data. A 2018 study found that Facebook owned the world's biggest data pool and "social graph" showing how its members are connected. When Caesars Entertainment, a casino group, went bankrupt in 2015, the data pool it had collected from its consumer loyalty program was valued by the bankruptcy auditors at a higher price than all of its properties on the Las Vegas strip. Your best strategy with "free" online services is take steps to avoid paying lock-in fees and to take precautions to monitor the personal data you share. If you can do this, then you can sit back and enjoy the satisfying consumer experience of using a new and engaging product for zero dollar cost.

Senior Discounts

Everyone is familiar with the senior citizen discount. Once you reach that magic age of 55 or so, you have the privilege of ordering from the menu section at your favorite restaurant that has special prices for "Our Honored Senior Guests." Charging different prices to different groups for essentially the same product is an everyday practice that we are so familiar with that we hardly think about it. There are senior citizen and student discount prices at movies, different prices for airline tickets depending on length of stay and time of purchase, a variety of greens fees on golf courses depending on the time of day and week, senior and child discount prices at amusement parks, and on and on. What is going on here? In particular, why do some sellers charge different prices to different groups of buyers while others do not?

The practice of charging different groups different prices for the same product is known as price discrimination. Movies are a great example that I expect you are quite familiar with. There can be a student price, children's price, senior price, military service price, daytime discount price, and, of course, the regular price. Now, why would a theater want to do such a thing? The answer, clearly, is that they hope to make more money this way. One factor at work is that the demand for a product may vary by the time of day, so it makes sense to charge a lower price in periods of low demand. The twilight price offered near the end of the day at golf courses fits here, as do daytime prices for movies. It is also clear that different groups of people have different abilities to pay for a good. Children have less to spend than adults, for example, as do full-time students compared to full-time working adults.

There is a general principle lying behind all of these practices. By charging different prices to different people for the same good, a seller is able to capture more of the value buyers get from buying the good. To see how this works, think back to our discussion of scalping and the idea that in voluntary market transactions almost everyone gets a "good deal" at the market price. This is because many people would have been willing to pay somewhat more for the good if they had to. The fact that there is only one market price allows these good deals to exist. Now suppose that a firm knows exactly what everyone really is willing to pay for their product and can make everyone pay exactly that price. If a firm could do this, it would make a lot more money because it would be capturing the "good deal" that most consumers get when there is only a single market price. Charging different prices to different groups by price discrimination is a strategy to try to get closer to this multiple-price result.

When can firms do such a thing? Restaurants, movies, planes, and buses do this. Yet clothing stores, supermarkets, and hardware stores do not. A place to start is to note that price discrimination cannot occur if buyers can readily switch to another seller to get the same good. So price-discriminating markets must have at least to some degree a limited numbers of sellers. If you want to travel by plane from Bellingham to Seattle in Washington State, you only have two airlines to choose from. If you want to go to that great first-run dinosaur disaster movie, you have to go to one of the few theaters in the area that is showing it. There cannot be multitudes of sellers of identical goods, in other words, to chose from.

These features are just as true of hardware stores and supermarkets as movies and restaurants, however, so something else must be at work. Two other features of markets are necessary for firms to practice successful price discrimination. First, sellers must be able to divide their buyers into identifiable groups that have different abilities to pay for their good. You surely remember how the idea of dividing buyers into groups worked when you went to movies as a kid. Children and senior citizens pay lower prices at movies because sellers know that these groups are in general less wealthy than prime-working-age adults. Charging these groups the normal adult fare would keep many of them from attending movies and cut the theaters off from a significant part of the market.

But even this is not enough to allow price discrimination. Facing distinct groups with differing abilities to pay also applies to hardware stores. So a final feature is necessary for effective price discrimination, and that is the inability of buyers of the good to resell it. After you go to a movie, it is pretty hard to sell the experience to someone else. The same is true of a plane trip or a round of golf. There is a possibility of buying the ticket and selling it to someone else, of course, but price discriminators think of this. This is why children's and senior's tickets at movies are clearly labeled, and why airlines examine customer identification at the check-in counter (for security reasons, to be sure, but the practice also neatly allows for the monitoring of ticket sales to be sure that the buyer of a ticket is actually the person who is taking the trip— check back and see how strongly airlines objected when the government imposed stricter identification rules on airline passengers). Disneyland Paris divided its buyers by charging different prices on its websites in different nations in Europe and making it difficult to access other national sites.

The example of the consumer electronics firm that prices its new devices high and then lowers the prices over time also fits here. The consumer electronics firms are actually using a price discrimination strategy that allows them to sell the same good to different people at different prices. Movie theaters and airlines sell their tickets to people who are using their product at the same time. To do this effectively they have to be able to prevent the resale of tickets from people who pay lower prices to those who pay the higher price. The beauty of the consumer electronics strategy is that they don't have to worry about resales because the groups who pay high and low prices are buying the product at different times. They sell the goods to those willing to pay a high price first and only later in time sell to those willing to pay a low price.

It is the difficulty of reselling many products that allows price discrimination to become a common practice. If resales are easy, then price discrimination will not work. If your local Ford dealer tried offering large student discounts, you would probably see a lot of students buying new Fords that somehow end up being driven by their relatives and neighbors. The same goes for supermarkets and hardware stores; the opportunity to resell goods bought in these places cannot be easily monitored. If hardware stores had large senior discounts, then grandmas would be doing a lot of buying of shovels and plumbing supplies that would end up at their grandkids' homes. Even these firms, however, will price discriminate where they have the chance of effectively monitoring the likelihood of resales. Car dealers may have special fleet rates when selling to large companies because they are guaranteed that the cars will be used for corporate use and not passed on to the general consumer market, and retail stores often give employee discounts backed by the threat of firing the employee if they abuse the privilege.

Because price discrimination can be lucrative, firms will do it if they can. In a study of final sales prices for new cars during the month of February 2000, David Harless and George Hoffer found strong evidence of extensive price discrimination among 2,300 auto dealers from across the country. They found particularly convincing evidence for discrimination among age groups and between those who pay cash or arrange their own financing, with older buyers paying more and those arranging their own financing paying less. Although they could not make a judgment on race in their data set, they found no evidence of discrimination against women.

Since price discrimination is profitable if it works, there are all kinds of examples of the practice. In a study of pricing policy by Amazon, *Los Angeles Times* reporter David Streitfeld found that the prices of books he listed in a shopping basket changed regularly by several percent. Puzzled by the changes, he decided to investigate what was going on. The people he interviewed guessed that Amazon was using a price discrimination program similar to those used by airlines in pricing airfares. A few years ago, the Coca-Cola Company even experimented with a vending machine that used heat sensors to change the price of a soda based on the air temperature. On a hot day, the price went up, and on cold days it went down. The howls of protest among consumers were so loud that the company decided to shelve the product.

Because price discrimination pays in terms of profits earned, firms spend a lot of time and effort thinking about ways they can do it. Airlines have departments headed by PhDs whose task is to monitor and adjust prices to get the most they can out of price discrimination. Some of the ways firms come up with to price discriminate are more subtle than directly charging different people different prices for the same good. If you have bought a printer for your computer, you probably noticed that the price of the printer seemed quite reasonable but the price of the ink cartridge was very high. This is actually a price discrimination scheme. Firms charge a low price for the printer in order to get one on your desk. Heavy users of the printer then buy a lot of cartridges and pay a lot in total. Light users of the printer use few cartridges and pay less. Firms don't just give the printer away, however, because savvy users can figure out lower-cost options to buying same-brand cartridges. Because selling cartridges is so profitable, printer firms go to great lengths to stop the use of other brands, including putting smart chips in their cartridges that make them harder to refill and sending software updates to their printers that disable machines without the correct cartridges. If printer firms could totally guarantee that you buy their cartridge, they would cut their printer prices to the bone. You actually see this done at times with some goods. Not long ago, for example, I received a new razor unsolicited in the mail. The razor firm was willing to give the razors away because they make their money on selling the high-priced blades. The price of blades is so high that the blade display in drug stores is often locked and requires a clerk's assistance to get the product.

You can even find the printer cartridge and razor blade strategy for price discrimination in some movie theaters. Many large cities have theaters that charge very low prices and may even have times when admission is free. These places do not show first-run films, of course, and, in fact, often specialize in much older, family-oriented films. When you walk into the theater, however, you will notice that it has a large, clean, and well-stocked concession stand. These theaters are doing what printer and razor makers are doing by charging a very low price for the basic good (in this case admission to the theater) and making their money from add-ons (in this case sales of popcorn, sodas, and candy).

When you come across a market as a consumer where firms are charging different people different prices for the same good because resales are not possible, the best strategy by far is to check to see if you are the member of one of the groups charged a lower price. These groupings can vary widely, including age, time of day, date of purchase, student status, military status, and membership in organizations like AAA, AARP, or your employer. When prices are publicly posted as in major movie theaters, this is not too difficult to do. Even then, however, not all discounts may be listed, and you may have to ask if your veteran status or AAA card gives you a better price. When prices are not publicly posted, the process may take a fair amount of effort. If you buy airline tickets online, for example, you probably have had the experience of spending a good amount of time sorting out the prices based on departure time, date of purchase, day of week, and connections. The difficulty of determining the actual price is illustrated most dramatically by goods like computer printers and men's razors, which make their money off the cartridges and blades that may be bought far in the future from the original purchase. As you will recall, computer printers were an example of goods with hidden prices. If the different prices being charged to different buyers vary widely, however, determining the groups you belong to is often well worth the effort.

College Grants

One fact that makes contemplating college tuition less painful is that you know that many colleges and universities have generous scholarship and grant programs to help bring the tuition price down. In an overview of the grant process, Richard McKenzie reported that a 2007 survey found that 95 percent of 107 private colleges and universities gave grants to over half of their students based on financial need. These grants are tuition reductions, so students who receive them pay a lower price to attend college. Because of the wide use of grants by college and universities, financial advisers tell students not to be put off by the listed prices of the colleges they are interested in. They tell them to apply and see what the college offers in grants and subsidies. The end result can be that attending a private college or university may be lower than attending a public one. Since so many students qualify for these tuition reductions, you may wonder why schools don't just lower the price and avoid all the hassle of filling out and evaluating all of the paperwork needed to award the grants.

The answer, it shouldn't be a surprise to know, is the same as for movie tickets, soft drinks, and consumer electronics. Colleges and universities know that some people are willing to pay a higher price than others for the services they offer and that people have a bias to buy more at a lower price. In fact, schools actually try to do a bit of both what consumer electronics sellers do and what movie ticket sellers do. The consumer electronics strategy, as you will recall, was to price high early in the offering of a product and to lower the price over time. The early admission programs that many colleges and universities offer allows them to do just that. Students who commit themselves in an early admission program state that they will attend the school and not consider other offers. McKenzie reports that as a result of these commitments, early admission students receive fewer grants and pay a higher tuition price than those not participating in the program.

Early admission students, of course, are not all of the students. For those who decide later, the schools rely on the movie ticket strategy. In order to charge different customers different prices for the same thing, movie theaters and airlines have to prevent resales. Movie theaters do this by printing different color tickets with bold lettering announcing that the buyer is a child or an adult. Airlines achieve this through the process of screeners matching every ticket to its buyer. The way colleges and universities do this is by tailoring every aid package individually for each student. Since the process and paperwork to do this is detailed, time consuming, and expensive, the fact that schools keep it up must mean the outcome is worth the cost. At the end, the process may mean that almost every student in the entering class in a small college pays an amount that is different from every other student.

Movie theaters and airlines are profit-making enterprises, so the extra money they earn through price discrimination becomes profit for company owners. The fact that most colleges and universities are not-for-profit institutions means that they are willing to go so far as charging some students amounts that do not even cover their costs. The higher amounts paid by students who receive small tuition reductions are used to pay for these low-fee students. The fact that the tuition paid is different for almost everyone also implies that there is room for negotiation on these prices. The fact that a college education is very expensive makes it inherently a negotiated price, but the individualized nature of tuition adds to the likelihood that there is some flexibility to work with. The individualized nature of the prices offered also explains why schools that are in high demand with large numbers of applicants do not offer anywhere close to the grant discounts of places that have fewer applicants. They don't have to lower the price to anyone because they can sell all they have to offer to those who are willing to pay more. In his review of the grant process, McKenzie reports that some schools even acknowledge the negotiable nature of their offers and cites Carnegie-Mellon University, which at one time included the sentence in letters to students, "If you received a financial-aid package from us that was not competitive with other offers, let us know."

Since college and universities are extensive users of pricing strategies, it shouldn't surprise you to know that they use the same ideas in other ways. Beside charging tuition, colleges and universities raise money by asking for gifts from alumni and other supporters. Giving money away is simply another way that you can choose to spend your income, just like going to a movie or buying a new pair of shoes. At first glance it would seem that the price of giving would only be the dollar amount you choose to part with. In fact, things are not so straightforward. Since most colleges and universities are not for profit, these are tax-deductible gifts. The tax deduction in effect lowers the cost of the gift, so it should not be a surprise that emphasizing the tax-saving nature of gifts is an important way that schools and other charities motivate people to give. As the friendly and helpful university gift solicitor will tell you, it may look like a $10,000 gift, but at your federal and state tax brackets it really will only cost you $7,000.

Are there any other ways to make charitable giving cost less? Dean Kaplan and John List were interested in this issue and explored the question of whether matching gifts also act to lower the price of giving. A matching gift is a situation where every dollar you give is "matched" at some level by another giver, with a $1:$1 match being very common. To test the influence of a match, Kaplan and List ran an experiment based on solicitation of funds from 50,000 prior donors. Individuals were randomly assigned to solicited groups with no matching funds and with matches at different levels. The overall result was that matching increased both the likelihood of giving and the amount donated. In their sample, the amount given increased by 19 percent, and the probability of giving rose by 22 percent in the groups where the match applied. Kaplan and List were careful to point out the limits of their study. In particular, it was for a political campaign, and the demand for giving may be different between those giving to colleges and political parties just like the demand is different for consumer electronics and Halloween candy. But the strength of the Kaplan and List results suggests that gift matches act just like lowering the price.

As you consider the challenge of paying for your own or your child's college education, it is probably not much comfort to know that the pricing practices of colleges and universities are based on the same type of demand analysis used by sellers of Halloween candy, french fries, airline tickets, consumer electronics, and movie tickets, but it does suggest some strategies for dealing with the situation. It is clear that there is room for negotiation in these prices, so it will be worth your time to pay close attention to the process. The fact that colleges and universities tailor their prices to fit the characteristics of individual students suggests as well that there is good reason to look broadly at college opportunities in order to have a good number of grant and subsidy possibilities to consider.

CHAPTER TEN

High-Paid Jobs, Tenure, and Why Are There So Many Lawyers?

Structural and Behavioral Factors in Labor Markets

The main source of income for most of us is what we earn at our job. Because that paycheck has to take care of almost everything, both while we are working and after we retire, labor market issues are of critical interest to almost everyone. It would be nice if labor markets were simple and straightforward like weekend yard sales, but when you hear or read about labor markets a host of seemingly haphazard practices appears to exist. I had a guest speaker in class, for example, who worked for a well-known firm. As she talked about conditions that existed in her industry, she said that one of the notable things about working for her firm was that it paid better than anywhere else. She said that people talked about being attached to the firm by "golden handcuffs"; people did not leave even if they did not like their job because the pay was so good. If you think about work and pay in your city, you know that some firms have the reputation of paying better than others for the same work, even if it seems that they don't have to. Why would they do this?

You also probably know that some jobs have "tenure," meaning that a job is essentially guaranteed in the future. University professors and public school teachers come to mind, but the same practice exists in other professions such as the requirement to "make partner" in a law firm or an accounting firm in order to move ahead in your job. Academic freedom is often given as the reason for granting tenure in universities, but this can't be true for essentially the same practice by accountants. Is there something more general about the features of certain kinds of labor markets that leads employers to, in effect, guarantee future employment?

You may also wonder at times about how people choose the work they do. Many people have talents of intelligence, industry, and ambition that can be used to advantage in many different occupations. Why do they choose to use their talents as they do? Why are there so many lawyers in the United States compared to Japan? Why do so many of the "best" people in developing countries seem to go into the armed forces or government? The general issue here is why talent is distributed the way it is in a given economy.

High-Paid Jobs

What makes a great job? To me, the list of features of an ideal job would include autonomy, flexibility, ease of commute, and pay—more or less in that order. By autonomy I mean whether someone is watching over your every move on the job. By flexibility I mean the pace and hours of work. Ease of commute refers to how much time and effort it takes to get to the workplace. And pay is, obviously, the price paid for your labor.

This list of features is purely personal and yours may be quite different. But I expect that your definition of a great job would also include a list of features beyond just the pay. This implies a couple of important things about prices in labor markets. One is that a great job is a "price-plus-other-features" good like a candy bar or a gift. As you will recall, the complete price of a candy bar is the price of the bar plus the time it takes to acquire it. As Henry David Thoreau put it in *Walden*, "the cost of a thing is the amount of what I will call life which is required to be exchanged for it." Thoreau's focus was on time, but other features of goods matter as well. In the case of gifts the total value is the price plus the sentiment attached to it. A gift with a dollar price of only pennies can be greatly valued if the circumstances are right. My wife and my father exchanged the same set of wooden pegs as birthday gifts for years, and both of them got enormous pleasure out of finding new ways to present their gifts each year.

Great jobs are "price-plus" goods like gifts and candy bars. In my case, autonomy, flexibility, and access are "plus" factors that matter. Others may place a high value on working for a place that has a prestigious name. The geographic location may matter most to some. Others may place more emphasis on the everyday environment on the job. A 2017 study of unskilled jobs, for example, found that the average worker was willing to give up 20 percent of their wage to avoid irregular work schedules set at short notice.

What this all adds up to, of course, is that the price paid for the work may in fact be secondary in how highly someone values a job. But that price does matter, and jobs do have different prices. Are there factors that matter here? Is there a checklist of characteristics that you can use to identify a high-paying job? Given the discussions in the previous chapters, it shouldn't be a surprise to learn that this is in fact the case. Some of these features are pretty obvious, but others are less well known. When you come across a job that has several of the features together, you will find that it can be very well paid indeed.

Let's start with an obvious fact that affects the price of a job. Simply put, firms do not hire workers just to have them around. Workers are hired to accomplish a specific task, and that task is related to the goods or services provided by the organization. This leads to the first feature of a high-paying job. Pay depends in a critical way on the price of the final goods or services the labor helps to produce. People who have jobs in rapidly growing and very profitable firms thus will tend to get paid more than people who do exactly the same work in firms that are stagnant and barely surviving.

The fact that firms hire workers to do a specific task leads to several other features of high-paid work. If a job is critically necessary to the production of the final good or service and the job cannot be eliminated, then it will tend to be paid higher. If labor costs are a small percentage of the total costs of providing the final goods or services of the organization, then work will tend to be paid more. If jobs are directly tied to operating expensive and necessary equipment or machinery, they will tend to be paid more. If a job requires a particular skill or training to produce at a high-quality level, it will tend to be paid more.

There are other pretty obvious factors that also influence pay. If a job is dangerous or safe, dirty or clean, permanent or seasonal, inside or outside, close-by or distant, then pay will tend to differ, with premiums paid for dangerous, dirty, seasonal, outside, and distant work. A temporary job working on cleaning up a remote hazardous waste site thus will tend to get paid more per hour than a permanent job cleaning up a local, safe site. Without knowing anything about the actual wage levels, I expect that the jobs involved in cleaning up nuclear waste at the Hanford Reservation site in Washington State pay pretty well.

These features of high-paid jobs are well known to anyone who has had experience in market economy labor markets. There are also several less obvious circumstances that matter in pay, including, for example, required credentials to get a job, the number of firms competing to hire workers, and the motivation and monitoring system used to supervise workers. Since these are less well-known factors in creating high-paid jobs, they are worth looking at in some detail.

The importance of required credentials in labor markets has received increasing attention in recent years. In the state of California, for example, there were 177 licensed occupations in the year 2007. In the same year in Arizona, which borders California, there were 72 licensed occupations. The reasons given for requiring a license to practice an occupation are usually about assuring public safety and improving product or service quality. This can certainly be true, but the practical effect of requiring a license is to raise the price of labor. A person working in an Arizona town on the border with California in one of the 105 jobs that required a license in California but not in Arizona could not get a job just across the border for exactly the same work without putting in the time, effort, and money to acquire the required license. Occupational licensing, in other words, keeps people out of competition for jobs, and this lack of competition can create higher pay. Morris Kleiner and Alan Krueger were curious about how great this impact can be and conducted a survey to find out. Their review of past studies found a range from 10 percent to 15 percent for higher wages due to occupational licensing. The results of their own 2008 survey showed even higher numbers, with 17 percent higher earnings associated with state-level licensing and nearly 25 percent higher pay for occupations that required both federal-level and state- or local-level licensing.

Kleiner and Krueger also found that the percentage of workers in jobs covered by occupational licensing laws had risen from less than 5 percent in the early 1950s to 25 percent in 2008. The fact that the percentage of the labor force in union jobs has moved in the reverse direction, falling from over 25 percent of private sector workers in the 1950s to less that 10 percent in 2010, suggests that occupational licensing quietly and without fanfare has replaced unionization as the method of choice by workers to band together to raise wages. Belonging to an occupation with strong licensing requirements can give workers the same wage and fringe benefits, sense of being a member of a special group, and solidarity of common interests as belonging to a union, but within a more white-collar, professional context.

By the late 2010s, awareness of the rise of occupational licensing had reached a level where it brought policy attention, with the Council of Economic Advisers (CEA) publishing a major study in 2015 of the trend and its effects and sponsoring congressional hearings on the topic in 2016. Interestingly, the proper role and extent of occupational licensing is an area of economic policy on which politicians from both the right and the left tend to agree. The concerns raised by the Democratic Obama CEA were picked up and carried forward in the Republican Trump administration by the Department of Labor and the Federal Trade Commission. All groups raised concerns about the inconsistencies and restrictions imposed by state policies that, as a 2017 article reported, required 1,825 hours of education and experience for a painting contractor in Arkansas and zero hours in Washington.

Another critical factor influencing pay is the number of firms that want to hire your labor. If there is only one potential employer for your work, that firm will tend to try to take advantage of the situation and pay you less. That this actually works in labor markets was shown dramatically in Major League Baseball when teams were forced to switch from exclusive contracts to free agency for their players. In the old system, the labor of a player was owned by one team. The player's choices were to settle, stay home, or find another occupation. Under free agency, when a player's contract ends, they can offer their labor to other teams in the leagues. That teams took advantage of contracts under the old system to keep salaries down was clearly shown when the exclusive contract restraints came off in the mid-1970s. Paul Sommers and Noel Quinton were interested in this impact and did a detailed study of the effects. In their work they found that from 1973 to 1975, just before the change, the average increase in baseball salaries was 0–2 percent per year. In 1976, the first year of free agency, the average increase was almost 10 percent and in 1977 it was 38 percent. Over the period of the transition to the new system, player salaries as a portion of team revenues rose from 17.6 percent in 1974 to 41.1 percent in 1982.

The same effects were found in a study of the *kafala* migrant worker system in the Middle East by Suresh Naidu, Yaw Nyarko, and Shing-Yi Wang. Under the system workers are tied to their employers even after their employment contracts expire. Under a 2010 reform, some *kafala* workers in the United Arab Emirates were allowed to look for work with other employers when their contracts ended. Naidu, Nyarko, and Wang found that real wages rose over 10 percent within three months for these workers and estimated that overall wages were 27 percent lower for migrant workers under the *kafala* system than if firms had to compete for their labor.

José Azar, Ioana Marinescu, and Marshall Steinbaum were interested in whether the relationship between restricted competition for workers and lower pay was broader than in just a few industries. Using data in a 2017 study for 8,000 geographic-occupational labor markets across the United States, they found that the average U.S. labor market was highly concentrated and that moving from the 25th percentile of concentration to the 75th percentile was associated with a 15–25 percent decline in wages. In a second paper, the same authors, along with Bledi Taska, found that 20 percent of all workers in the United States worked in highly concentrated labor markets.

Taking a different approach to the issue of restricted competition for workers, other late 2010s studies have found that about 20 percent of all U.S. workers are covered by noncompete clauses in their employment contracts. These requirements state that employees cannot work for competing firms for a set amount of time. The requirements make sense for jobs that involve knowing trade secrets or other confidential information. When they apply to fast food workers, as they did for employees at Wendy's, Arby's, Burger King and other chains in the 2010s, it is hard to explain their purpose in any reasonable way other than as attempts to limit the competition for workers in their labor markets. As the changes in the baseball and *kafala* markets show, more competition for workers in labor markets tends to lead to higher pay.

How worker performance is supervised is another feature of labor markets that matters for pay levels. This feature is related to our old friend imperfect information. In particular, employers are not always able to know whether their employees are working hard at their jobs. In the terminology of the subject, there is a "monitoring" problem in many employment situations. What this means can be seen by considering different pay systems. Assume for the moment that you are a student living in an orchard region and are looking for a summer job picking cherries. You find two orchards with openings, one where you get paid by the weight of the cherries you pick and the other where you get paid by the hour. The first system is a piece-rate pay system. Under such a system, monitoring of worker performance is not much of an issue. In this case, the firm just weighs and pays (although the employer still needs to be sure that the cherries are being handled correctly and that workers are not in the habit of hiding a rock or two in their boxes to raise the weights). Under such a piece-rate payment system, a worker gets paid according to the amount he produces; if he works harder and more efficiently, he will make more money per hour.

Under most hourly-wage and salary systems, however, the connection between pay and production is not as direct. Again considering the cherry case, if the orchardist pays by the hour, she may find that workers have a tendency to work less hard than she wishes at the task they are hired to do. As the phrase goes, they tend to shirk at their work. If this is true, the employer will search for some way to encourage workers to produce at an acceptable level. One solution is to create a monitoring system that directly measures output. Many jobs that are tied to computers have built-in monitoring systems: grocery checkers who use scanners, retail clerks who enter employee identification numbers when they ring up sales, and bank telephone-service representatives all can have their output easily quantified and compared to their coworkers and to firm standards. New technologies are created all the time that can be used to monitor work. Satellite positioning systems in vehicles can be used, for example, to monitor the progress of truck drivers or the location of police officers. Such information about the connection between time and effort, however, is not easily attainable for many jobs.

One possible solution to the problem of a lack of information about worker effort is for the firm simply to pay its employees very well. In cases where monitoring is expensive and where workers have a tendency to shirk, paying workers at rates significantly above what they could earn elsewhere could be used to encourage greater work intensity. Offering above-normal pay scales, as analyzed by Carl Shapiro, Joseph Stiglitz, George Akerlof, Janet Yellen, and others, has become known as the strategy of paying "efficiency wages." The term refers to the idea that firms pay workers well in order to encourage greater effort in their work.

Why would efficiency wages do the trick? From the workers' point of view, if they know that their pay is significantly above what they could earn at their best alternative elsewhere, they will not want to lose their job. The best way to keep their great-paying position is to work hard and be a good employee. Workers perform well, then, not because they are constantly monitored but because of their personal interest in keeping their job.

Do firms actually do this, and does it in fact work? The answers to these questions appear to be yes, and yes. There clearly are firms that tie their employees to their jobs with "golden handcuffs." The whole notion of efficiency wages was invented as an explanation for such cases. Broad studies of large groups of firms also find evidence that the practice is fairly widespread. A study by David Fairris and Lee Alston, for example, of national data on white male, nonunion, blue-collar production workers, working full-time in the private, nonagricultural sector, found evidence for efficiency wages in a distinct link between worker intensity and higher pay. Another study by Shailendra Raj Mehta found that paying high-efficiency wages was particularly likely in the most prosperous firms. Mehta concluded that this connection was due to the fact that managers' time is more valuable at prosperous firms, thus the cost of using that time to monitor workers is higher, and it becomes cheaper to just pay workers more to encourage self-motivation and reduce supervision time. Daniel Raff and Larry Summers have argued that the $5 per day pay introduced by Henry Ford in 1914, well above what workers could earn elsewhere, was an efficiency wage.

The idea behind efficiency wages can be extended to explain the practice of seniority pay. In a seniority system, workers who have been with a firm for a long time get paid more than those who have only worked for a short period, even though both long-term and short-term employees may be doing exactly the same job. Public school teachers are a good example, as are many production jobs. Now, it seems reasonable that a long-time teacher may well do his job better because of his years of experience. On many school district pay scales, however, long-term teachers make twice as much or more as beginners, a gap that seems too large based on experience alone. Why the large seniority differentials? The efficiency-wage explanation is that seniority pay scales are set up so that workers are actually underpaid relative to their productivity during their early years and overpaid during their later years. Employees who work in such a system know quite well that it works this way. They are encouraged to work hard by the fact that they will reap substantial rewards in time by a career of good performance and dedicated effort.

What all this comes down to is that there is a distinctive list of market features that create high-paying jobs. If pay is what matters to you, then look for a job that is in an organization that is profitable, that is growing rapidly, where labor is a small percentage of total costs, where labor is a necessity that cannot easily be replaced, where the job is attached to valuable equipment or technology, where the job requires skill or training, where a license or other credential is required, where there are multiple employers for your labor, that uses an efficiency-wage system, and, if you want to add all the components that might matter, the job is dangerous, dirty, temporary, outside, and requires a long commute. Not all of these features are needed, of course, to create a high-paying job, and probably there is no single job that has all of them, but this is a good checklist to have in mind if high pay matters to you.

It's good to know that pay tends to vary in an understandable way based on the conditions surrounding a job, but that doesn't help you much when you face the problem of finding a job in the first place. Is there anything useful to know about the task of getting hired? Actually, there are a couple of things that may be helpful. The first thing to keep in mind is that applying for a job is fundamentally about closing an information gap. We have seen how information gaps create issues for consumers in many everyday markets, from buying used cars, to dealing with experts, finding an ideal gift, or having to deal with a scalper to get a ticket to that great upcoming concert. Information gaps create the same kinds of issues in labor markets as they do in consumer markets. As you will recall, the information issue in the used car market was that sellers had information that buyers did not. In the case of labor markets, both buyers and sellers lack information that is important. As a potential employee, you certainly would like to know more about the quality and conditions of the work you are applying for. From the employer's point of view, he or she has a job that needs to be done but lacks thorough information about the applicants for the job.

As a result of the information gap they face when hiring workers, employers have an incentive to collect all the information they can that might indicate the character and personal qualities of applicants. This includes résumés and letters of recommendation, of course, but also credit histories, criminal records, drug tests, aptitude tests, personality tests, and online social media profiles. Because this information can be used to eliminate applicants for consideration for a job, some cities and states have banned the use of drug tests, credit checks, or criminal histories from employment interviews. The unintended effect of these prohibitions, however, has been to reduce the probability of black workers being employed. A study of credit record bans found that black employment fell by up to a sixth, a study on drug tests found allowing such tests raised black employment by up to 30 percent, and one on criminal records found that banning the use of this information reduced the probability of blacks being employed by over 5 percent. With less information, apparently employers are more restrictive in their hiring decisions, and this restriction works to the disadvantage of minority groups.

What this means for you as a potential employee is that what you need to do is to explain as specifically and clearly as possible to the employer why you can do the job available and how you have the qualities that the employer is looking for. You probably remember hearing advice to familiarize yourself with a company and its work before you apply for a job. With the idea of closing an information gap in mind, you can see how good that advice is. If you gather that information, not only will you know more that is useful to you about the qualities and conditions of the work, but you can explain much better why you are the best applicant for the job.

The second thing to keep in mind when you are applying for jobs is the list of characteristics that create good paying jobs. These features, which include occupational licensing, firms that are highly profitable and growing rapidly, and working with valuable equipment, can be summarized by recalling some investment advice from Warren Buffet. When looking for a good investment opportunity, Buffet has said that he looks for strong companies with "a moat around them." If you are looking for a good job, you should do the same thing and look for jobs with a moat around them. These moats can be around the job itself (such as an occupational license or required skills) or around the firm (firms with high profits and growth or legal protections from competition). These features protect a job from forces that create low pay and insecurity.

The ideas of information gaps and moats also help explain why earning a college degree is worth so much. A completed degree provides information to an employer about your qualifications for a job. To complete a college degree takes planning, organization, a sense of purpose, and personal responsibility. By completing the degree, you indicate to an employer that you have the abilities and personal qualities needed to complete a complex and difficult task.

If you keep in mind the ideas of information gaps and moats, the process of looking for a job can be a bit less intimidating. It makes it more practical and impersonal. You will still have a lot of work to do to find out about the expectations of the jobs you apply for and to figure out how best to close the information gap that employers have about you as a job candidate. But if you glance from time to time at a piece of paper in your pocket that says "information gaps" and "job moats" as you apply for jobs, you can better keep a focus on things that matter for the task at hand. It will help you collect and organize the information you need in a job search and will suggest the kinds of questions you need to ask as you go about the process.

Tenure

Most universities and colleges have a tenure system where faculty, after a period of several years, are awarded a position of "continuous appointment" if they meet certain criteria. The practice of tenure is also a feature of many partnerships in law, accounting, and other professions; if an employee does not "make partner" after a certain time, they are let go or frozen in dead-end, low-pay jobs. The guarantee under such systems is strong but not absolute; tenured university faculty can be let go during periods of financial crisis or for serious violations of professional standards.

Why this strong commitment to job security after some point in time? As explained in a discussion of tenure by Paul Milgrom and John Roberts, a primary reason is due to a special kind of imperfect information in labor markets. In particular, in some professions the best judges of the quality of applicants for a position are the colleagues with whom they will be working. Say a university has a position open for an applied microeconomist specializing in industrial organization. Who will be the best judge of the qualifications of candidates? The dean, with her PhD in mathematics? The Faculty Personnel Committee, with representatives from geology, English, art history, and political science? Or the members of the economics department, especially the other applied microeconomists?

The answer is clear; because of the specialized professional knowledge required in the position, the candidate's future colleagues are best able to evaluate his or her qualifications. This, then, can create a problem, because economics department members are in effect recruiting their own potential replacements. Assume there is no tenure and it becomes necessary to cut an economist or two. Who will the dean let go? A strong incentive for the administration will be to fire the least competent faculty first (which could be the least published, the most out of date in their technical abilities, or the least effective teacher, depending on what kind of performance the university values). In such a situation, the incentive for faculty when they hire new colleagues will be to choose less able candidates. By doing so they will protect themselves when job reductions come around.

Tenure changes these incentives. If they have tenure, current faculty will have little to fear from hiring new colleagues who are the best available. In fact, if faculty reductions are made, as they usually are in university tenure systems, by eliminating entire departments rather than reducing the size of several areas, then the incentive of existing faculty will be to hire the very best colleagues they can get. By hiring the best colleagues, faculty create strong departments. This will help protect them if reductions in faculty size become necessary.

Tenure, then, is a way to ensure that the best person is hired for a job in situations where colleagues are the best judges of candidate qualifications. This seems to apply best to situations where specialized professional knowledge is necessary to evaluate candidates. Law and accounting partnerships apply here as well as colleges and universities. As a concluding note, as Milgrom and Roberts point out, tenure also has the positive effect of making everyone take employee evaluations very seriously. Since the tenure decision is so important, those involved pay great attention to regular reviews of employee performance.

Why Are There So Many Lawyers?

Articles commonly appear comparing the number of lawyers in different countries—or the number of engineers, government employees, entrepreneurs, or school teachers. These are interesting details. But the broader issue behind these facts is the question of what causes people to pick one career over another in a country.

Clearly, not all workers are alike. One result is that not everyone will be paid the same because pay will tend to be higher for those with better talents. As a result, people with ability and talent will have an incentive to search for occupations that reward their skills the most. Some talents are very specific—such as the ability to throw a baseball accurately 100 miles per hour—so the choice of occupations will be limited. Many other talents, however, are quite general in their applications. A combination of intelligence, a good sense of responsibility, the ability to get along well with other people, and a strong work ethic can lead to success in a wide variety of fields. In some countries a lot of these people will become lawyers (or government bureaucrats or entrepreneurs), while in other countries very few will choose these jobs. What explains the distribution of occupations chosen by people with strong general talents?

An article by Kevin Murphy, Andrei Shleifer, and Robert Vishny considers this issue in detail and concludes that there are three key factors at work affecting the distribution of talent. The first factor is the size of the market. If your career choices are to be the best corncob pipe whittler in the United States or the twentieth-best professional golfer, you almost certainly will stick with the little white ball and put the knife aside. The market for hand-whittled corncob pipes is not a large one, while millions can be earned playing golf even if you are only the twentieth-best. The second key factor Murphy, Shleifer, and Vishny found was how many money-making transactions can be taken care of by the same person. A successful doctor can only see so many patients in a day, but a famous writer can sell the same work to hundreds of thousands of readers. The third factor was how much of the income that they generate can be captured by a worker. More people will tend to become novelists if writers on average receive 80 percent of the cover price of their books than if they only receive 5 percent.

Clearly, this argument by Murphy, Shleifer, and Vishny is directly connected to our earlier discussions of superstars and moats around jobs. Superstars earn gigantic salaries in areas with large markets and where they can capture a good share of the income they generate. Murphy, Shleifer, and Vishny focus on the more general point, however, that because of legal and social structures different occupations in different countries will have the "right" set of characteristics that attract large numbers of talented people. In other words, different jobs in different countries will have protected moats around them.

The authors use the example of Talleyrand in the eighteenth century, who was a bishop in France with a large tax-revenue income before becoming an entrepreneur with a large profit income in the United States. Occupational characteristics at the time were such that men of talent were attracted into the church in France and into business in the United States. For the same reason, there is an abundance of lawyers in the United States today compared to the number in Japan.

This is more than just an interesting detail about why occupations are more popular in some nations than in others. As Murphy, Shleifer, and Vishny point out, the resulting distribution of talent matters for such critical issues as economic growth and the national standard of living. If employment conditions are such that most of the people with talent choose occupations that add to production, then growth and increases in living standards may occur faster than if people choose jobs that merely redistribute income from one group to another. From this point of view, social and economic incentives that make careers as entrepreneurs or engineers attractive will enhance growth more than incentives that lead people to choose careers as investment bankers, lawyers, government bureaucrats, or army officers. In their empirical tests, Murphy, Shleifer, and Vishny found that countries that had a high proportion of engineering graduates grew faster than nations with a high proportion of law students.

The idea that people choose occupations where they can do best has other implications as well. One interesting area is the choice of jobs by men and women. As discrimination based on sex has declined within nations, the performance of boys and girls on standardized test scores has changed. A study of results on standardized test scores from exams given to 270,000 students in forty countries found that as gender equality improved within nations, the differences in math scores between fifteen-year-old boys and girls disappeared. At the same time, the gap between boys' and girls' reading scores increased, with girls pulling farther ahead of boys. One expectation of improvements in gender equality has been that women would move more strongly into occupations in math and science. This has not happened at the expected rate, however, which has led to speculation about factors at work. Some say it is social factors, such as lingering sex discrimination among the male-dominated math and science professions. According to Paola Sapienza, one of the authors of the study on boys' and girls' exam scores, the reason may be more about economics. If gender equality means that boys and girls have equal abilities in math and science but that girls have a large advantage in reading skills, then girls will choose to do what they can do the best. Just like Talleyrand changed occupations when he moved from France to the United States, girls will do the same when they make their career choices. Rather than studying math and science, they may choose law.

CHAPTER ELEVEN

Beauty, Orchestra Auditions, and the Rat Race

Behavioral Biases and Information Gaps in Labor Markets

When you are looking for a job, you probably wonder at times about the fairness of the process. You know that in the past discrimination on the basis of race, gender, or religion was common, and you wonder how things have changed in these supposedly more enlightened times. You also wonder about what conditions at the job will be like. You know that some places have the reputation of treating employees better than others, and you worry, quite rightly, about whether the pressures of the job will be good for you.

In looking at labor markets, researchers have asked the same kinds of questions about discrimination and work practices. In an attempt to go to the heart of what seems to many to be among the most arbitrary of practices in labor markets, Daniel Hamermesh and Jeff Biddle have conducted studies on the impact of physical appearance on earnings. In another study using data generated by a change in audition practices in the market for symphony orchestra musicians, Claudia Goldin and Cecilia Rouse looked for evidence of sex discrimination in hiring. It probably won't come as much of a surprise to learn that both studies found evidence of these biases. In terms of job conditions, Renée Landers, James Rebitzer, and Lowell Taylor looked into job pressures and identified features of work practices that may cause employees to work much harder and longer than they would under different circumstances.

Beauty and the Labor Market

A central feature of labor markets, certainly, is that not all workers are alike. As a result, it is not a great surprise—nor, actually, of much concern—that workers get paid differently depending on their talents and skills. Another feature of labor markets is that entry into specific labor markets is often quite difficult. The realities of acquiring desired talents and skills—some you are born with and some require long periods of expensive training and education—make us accept, perhaps grudgingly, that large pay differences between individual jobs can persist over time.

All of this makes outcomes in labor markets hard enough to deal with. But when people are paid differently according to personal characteristics that have nothing to do with job performance—such as their sex, race, or age—we tend to draw the line. Heaven knows that it is tough enough to do well in the U.S. labor force without bearing a burden of arbitrary treatment based on irrelevant personal features. For reasons of fairness and equity, discrimination based on such characteristics has been illegal in the United States for a good amount of time.

But we also know that habits of discrimination die hard. Because labor markets are not perfect, hiring and paying on the basis of personal characteristics still exists. Callback studies, where fictitious résumés for identically qualified candidates are sent to employers, have found that identical résumés using Asian-sounding names are 30 percent less likely to receive return calls. Black-sounding names are 50 percent less likely to receive a call. When Asian and black candidates removed all racial cues from their applications, they were twice as likely to get callbacks.

In an attempt to get a sense of what is happening in one of the seemingly most arbitrary areas of pay differentials, Daniel Hamermesh and Jeff Biddle have conducted studies about the effect of beauty in the labor market. Their purpose was quite straightforward—to see if there was evidence of preferential pay to those judged to be "good looking" or "strikingly handsome" in looks, or pay penalties to those judged to be "plain" or "homely."

The biggest challenge to doing such a study would seem to be finding data sets that provide information on pay and "looks." Interestingly enough, Hamermesh and Biddle found three such sources, two in Canada and one in the United States, which provided enough information for them to draw some conclusions. In these data, they found convincing evidence for a pay premium for better-than-average looks and a pay penalty for below-average looks.

Beyond this general conclusion, Hamermesh and Biddle found some interesting patterns. Somewhat surprisingly—given what most people would expect—both the pay premium and the pay penalty were greater for men than for women. Their conclusion was that the pay premium for good looks for men was 5 percent and the penalty 9 percent. For women, the premium was 4 percent and the penalty 6 percent. As these numbers show, there was a suggestion in the data that below-average looks received a larger penalty than the good-looks premium, but this result was not strong enough for certainty. Also of interest was the fact that both the premium and the penalty for beauty were not large. Although not trivial, the impact on earnings of looks was less than that found in other studies for gender, education, or race.

Because of the strength of the beauty effect, Hamermesh later tested his results by conducting studies using data from other places and times. In this work he found the same patterns of premiums for beauty and penalties for below-average looks. In Shanghai, China, the premium for men was 3 percent and the penalty 25 percent, while for women the data showed a premium of 10 percent and a penalty of 31 percent. Thus women faced a larger beauty effect than men compared to the United States, where the situation was reversed. In Britain, the beauty premium was the same for both men and women at 1 percent, but men did worse, with a negative 18 percent, than women, at negative 11 percent.

After finding that these effects exist, in their original study Hamermesh and Biddle then turned to the question of causes. After reviewing a variety of possibilities, they found modest support for the possibility that above-average-looking people tend to go into occupations where good looks pay off (sales for men; cashiers, receptionists, and waitresses for women). The effects here were weak, however. Their main conclusion about causes was that the main force at work appeared to be discrimination based on personal appearance and employer tastes.

This raises the question of whether beauty can be bought. The fact that the cosmetics industry has total world sales on the order of $300 billion annually certainly suggests that people try. Hamermesh tried to get a handle on this question in his Shanghai study, where the beauty effects were the greatest. The good news was that spending on beauty did have an effect. The bad news was that this spending did not have enough of an effect to pay for itself. In his study, the gains reflected in the beauty premium only covered 15 percent of the amount paid.

The pay premium for good looks raises the question, of course, of why this is the case. The Hamermesh and Biddle conclusion that discrimination was a factor encouraged other researchers to see if something else may be at work. To try and answer this question, Mark Prokosch, Ronald Yeo, and Geoffrey Miller conducted studies looking for links between physical features and scores on intelligence tests. In a related study, Gillian Rhodes and Leslie Zebrowitz surveyed the literature and created experiments where photographs of people who had taken intelligence tests were ranked by other people by beauty and by perceived intelligence. Other researchers have examined the connections between how people look and their health. The results of these studies imply that physical features actually do reflect underlying characteristics like intelligence and health. Not all of the pay differences that Hamermesh and Biddle found, in other words, appear to be due to discrimination. If good looks mean that people really do have traits that make them better employees, then it makes sense to pay them more.

This still, however, leaves an element of discrimination in pay based on looks alone. In suggesting earlier that keeping the ideas of information gaps and moats around jobs in mind can help in making a job search less intimidating, we focused on structural factors in a job search that you have some control over. The fact of discrimination suggests that there are behavioral features that we have less control over that affect job markets as well. Behavioral factors, as you will recall, are the attitudes, tendencies, and biases that we bring to economic decisions. In consumer markets, we found that attitudes about ownership, about the future, and about the status quo have important consequences on everyday markets and prices. The fact that these behavioral factors exist as well in labor markets probably should not be a surprise.

The evidence on discrimination based on good looks shows that employers have attitudes and biases about potential workers that they bring to the hiring decision. One way to summarize these attitudes is to think of them as the "family-and-friends" components of a job. The jobs we have say a lot about who we are both to other people and to ourselves and carry with them a host of connections and relationships with others. Since most of us care about these personal implications and connections, our attitudes about these issues get reflected in how job markets work. One way this happens is through attempts to reserve jobs with the best connections and best relationships for people with family-and-friends characteristics. The biases and behaviors based on these practices make up a good part of the elements of hiring and promotion in job markets that we tend to think of as unfair because they have little to do with the ability to do the job. Discrimination based on beauty, gender, race, sexual preference, religion, immigration status, or other factors belongs here, but so do practices such as giving preference in hiring or promotion to relatives, friends, and people with social, political, business, or school connections. In effect, discrimination and these other practices build a moat around a job that cannot be crossed unless you are a member of the relevant family-and-friends group.

If you have any contact with job markets at all, you know that these things matter. The children of well-connected individuals do not seem to have any trouble in finding good job opportunities, and if you happen to be in the final candidate pool for a job along with one of these people you know that you are probably out of luck. Because of the unfairness of hiring and promotion based on personal characteristics that have little or nothing to do with job performance, there are laws about many of these practices. Despite these controls, as the callback studies and as Hamermesh and Biddle found, behavioral biases still have effects on labor markets in the same way that they do in consumer markets. These behavioral biases are too powerful to legislate away completely.

Orchestra Auditions

When Hamermesh and Biddle stated in their study of the effects of beauty in labor markets that the best explanation for their findings was discrimination, they had no direct evidence for this conclusion. As you might guess, finding specific, direct evidence of discrimination based on non-work-related personal characteristics is pretty hard to do. Few people would ever admit to doing such a thing, and certainly no one is going to keep an explicit record of such practices.

Claudia Goldin and Cecilia Rouse, however, examined a set of data that provides unusually direct evidence of discrimination. They found that detailed records exist going back for decades of the hiring records of symphony orchestras. What makes these records interesting is that the hiring practices of orchestras changed significantly over time, as has the percentage of women who are hired. Taking into account other factors that have been at work—such as an increase in the number of women in the candidate pool for orchestra positions—Goldin and Rouse conclude that the change in hiring procedures accounts for about one-third of the increase in women among new hires. The low percentage of women hired before the hiring process change thus appears to be directly due to sex discrimination.

In the past, new members of major symphony orchestras tended to be handpicked by their music directors. In this system, those hired tended to be the students of a select group of teachers. In order to broaden the hiring process, during the 1970s and 1980s most orchestras began advertising new positions widely and hiring by auditions before committees. This made the process more open, but it did little to stop bias in hiring because prospective new hires could still be identified by sight and by name. The next step in the evolution of hiring procedures was to turn to blind auditions, where anonymous candidates would perform short preselected pieces behind screens. Goldin and Rouse found that most symphony orchestras changed to a version of this hiring process by the end of the 1980s.

At the same time that these changes in hiring procedures took place, there was a substantial rise in the percentage of women hired by major U.S. symphonies. In 1970, according to data compiled by Goldin and Rouse, the number of women who were members of the top five orchestras in the United States ranged from 2 percent to 12 percent. In 1990 the number ranged from 19 percent to 26 percent. Among the second tier of orchestras, the number of women who were members of four major symphonies in 1970 ranged from 11 percent to 19 percent, and from 18 percent to 38 percent in 1990. Given that the turnover among members of major orchestras is very low (around 5 percent in an average year), the percentage of women among new hires has been very high in order to cause these changes (the female share of new hires ranged from 26 percent to 60 percent among the top five orchestras in 1990).

Given these facts, Goldin and Rouse considered a range of possible causes for the increase in the percentage of women hired by orchestras. It wasn't due to an increase in the size of orchestras, for example, or a shift in their composition toward instruments more traditionally played by women. There have been no changes here in decades. They did find that the number of women who were candidates for positions had increased because of a rise in the percentage of women among music school graduates. But taking this and other changes into account did not explain all the increase in the percentage of women hired. Being conservative in their judgments, Goldin and Rouse at the end concluded that the switch to blind auditions accounted for 30 percent of the rise in the percentage of women among new hires and 25 percent of the increase in the percentage of women in the orchestras in their sample between 1970 and 1996.

The good news found by Goldin and Rouse was that the practices and consequences of gender discrimination in musician selection for orchestras were well in the past. The other good news was that eliminating these practices can have large and fairly rapid effects. The magnitudes they found in these changes showed how effective the moats around a job can be when selection based on family-and-friends factors not related to performance on the job are allowed to work.

It would be nice to believe that sexism in employment is all in the past, but we know that is not true. A careful study of student evaluations of male versus female professors at a university in the Netherlands covering the period 2009–2013 found that female professors were systematically and significantly rated lower by students. The class materials and readings used by female professors were rated lower even when they were identical to those used by their male peers. These evaluations matter, of course, in making decisions about promotion and pay. Evidence of continuing sexism in labor markets was also shown in a 2017 study by Alice Wu of online comments about male and female job candidates in the economics profession. The source was an online informal forum about gossip and rumor associated with the annual economics job market. The top thirty words associated with discussions of men and women candidates were totally different. The posts concerning women were far more frequently about appearance or personal characteristics while those about men were professionally and academically oriented. It is probably not a surprise to learn that the issues women face in receiving equal treatment in the job market in economics get reflected in their experiences once they have a job. A study by Erin Hengel found that the average time from submission to publication for women in economics is two years while the average time for men is eighteen months. This delay matters because tenure, promotion, and pay in the field are closely tied to the number and frequency of publications.

The best answer to all these issues is more and better information. Once these biases are exposed, steps can be taken to remedy them. When Alice Wu, the author of the article on words used to describe women versus men in the economics job market, was asked if her results discouraged her from pursuing a career in the field, her answer was no. She felt that her results implied, in fact, "that more women should be in this field changing the environment."

The Rat Race

Hiring and promotion are two areas of concern when you enter the labor force. An equally important one is conditions on the job. You probably have noticed that workers seem to work much harder at some jobs and in some firms than they do at others. Some places seem to be a real "rat race." Is there anything special going on in these jobs? Renée Landers, James Rebitzer, and Lowell Taylor were interested in this question and looked in detail at conditions that can turn a job into one characterized by long hours and intense effort.

Landers, Rebitzer, and Taylor looked at work hours in law firms to follow up on an idea suggested earlier by George Akerlof. According to Akerlof, excessive hours can exist in a work situation if there is a particular breakdown in information. We have found earlier that information gaps can cause several effects in markets. Fashion good markets have the price cycles they do because sellers do not have complete information about the tastes and preferences of their buyers. The market for used cars, on the other hand, has just the opposite problem, where sellers have more information about the characteristics of the cars they are selling than do buyers. Akerlof pointed out, as we discussed earlier, that a similar information gap exists in labor markets. In particular, employers wish to hire workers with certain characteristics, such as honesty, self-direction, and willingness to work hard. Potential employees know if they possess these characteristics, but employers do not. The result is an asymmetry in the information that employers and employees possess in the labor market, with buyers of labor not having complete information about their employees.

Landers, Rebitzer, and Taylor found that the particular structure of promotion and pay in law firms combines with this asymmetry in information to create a situation where hours worked can be excessively long by any reasonable standard. They found, in particular, that there is almost always some form of revenue sharing among partners in law firms. As a result, the income of any one partner is dependent to a degree on how much money his or her partner's earn for the firm. In such a situation partners have strong incentives to admit to partnership only those people who will be excellent income generators. The question facing partners as they consider an associate for advancement to partnership is thus how to know if he or she will in fact be a major money earner. Because there is no way to know about the existence of these personal characteristics with certainty, Landers, Rebitzer, and Taylor argue that partners look for good indicators of future productivity. The indicator they found that partners tend to use to screen candidates for the right kind of behavior is hours of work. Associates figure this out, of course, so the tendency is for candidates for partnership to work longer hours than they would choose to do so under different employment (but equal income) circumstances in order to show that they measure up to income-earning expectations. The partners, in turn, know the associates have figured this out, so the partners increase their expectations for hours worked even more in order to weed out those who are camouflaging their real work characteristics. The end result is a job pattern of excessively long work hours.

As a test of their argument, Landers, Rebitzer, and Taylor surveyed partners and associates at two large law firms. When they asked associates what they would choose if given the option for the coming year of keeping work hours constant with a 5 percent raise, reducing work hours by 5 percent with no change in income, or increasing hours by 5 percent with a 10 percent rise in income, nearly two-thirds of those responding said they would prefer to reduce their work hours. This was the result they expected if their argument was correct that workers were working longer than preferred hours because hours worked was being used as an indicator of willingness to work long, hard, and effectively. As another test of their argument, Landers, Rebitzer, and Taylor asked the associates in their sample what they would choose to do if the majority of associates in their firm increased their work hours by 5 percent. Again consistent with their argument, a substantial number of associates responded that they would choose to increase their hours as well.

The combination of asymmetry in labor market information, the revenue-sharing structure of law firms, and partners' tendency to use hours of work as an indicator for associates' ability to be future income generators creates a "rat race" of excessively long hours. Looking around for other similar labor situations, Landers, Rebitzer, and Taylor hypothesize that similar features may characterize work situations in major consultancies, academic departments in research universities, and in the competition for high-level managerial positions.

In discussing the hiring process earlier, we emphasized the importance of the information gap between employers and employees and suggested that an important strategy in looking for a job is to keep the information problem in mind so you can focus your attention on how to close the gap. What Landers, Rebitzer, and Taylor point out is that information gap problems carry over into the evaluation of your performance once you have the job. Almost every job you get will have some sort of evaluation process for employees. As Landers,

Rebitzer, and Taylor suggest, these evaluation systems have consequences. The goal of a firm is to have a fair, equitable, and easily understood evaluation system, but mistakes can be made. It is not hard to find examples. Microsoft, for instance, used a forced ranking system for several years where a given percentage of each work group was ranked each year at the bottom of a five-category scale. These employees could not keep their current positions and had to search for a new job elsewhere inside or outside of the firm. The system created widespread dissatisfaction among workers, in large part because of the inequity of applying the forced ranking to every group, whether everyone in the group was a truly excellent employee or everyone was actually below average. When these consequences became clear, the system was dropped. Even worse consequences occurred at Wells Fargo Bank when the bank created an employee evaluation system that rewarded the opening of new accounts. The result was that employees created literally millions of fake accounts to meet their employment goals. When the consequences of the evaluation system were revealed in 2016, the head of the company, other senior executives, and thousands of employees lost their jobs.

The information gap problem that Landers, Rebitzer, and Taylor examine in the evaluation of law firm employees is an example of a general kind of asymmetric information that can exist in contractual agreements. In the case of employment, an employee can have characteristics that are harmful for the employer that are not known when the employment contract is signed. Another common example where this occurs is insurance, where people who are most in need of health care are more likely to buy health insurance and people whose homes are most likely to be damaged by natural disasters are most likely to buy house insurance. Insurance companies know that this information gap exists, and thus they take measures to protect themselves, by writing exclusions, for example, into homeowner policies.

Another kind of information problem can also appear in contractual markets. As we just found, in the case of new lawyers the firm may not know something harmful about the worker when partnership is granted. It is also possible that one of the parties in a contract can change his or her behavior in a harmful way after the contract is signed. A classic example is the professional athlete who works hard and builds a great record, only to fall off noticeably in performance after signing that big-bucks, long-term, guaranteed contract. You probably don't have to think too long about the recent history of your favorite professional sport to come up with a name or two that applies. The savings-and-loan industry collapse of the 1980s, which you may recall cost U.S. taxpayers hundreds of billions of dollars to clean up, has also been attributed to this same problem. In the savings-and-loan case, after a major rewriting of federal rules affecting the financial industry in the early 1980s, dozens of institutions that had their deposits newly insured changed their behavior and started making risky loans and investments that eventually caused their bankruptcy.

As the law firms and Wells Fargo examples show, the problems caused by information gaps in labor markets are not confined just to hiring decisions. The whole process of promotion and motivation of existing employees has the same kind of information issues. Some firms purposely keep information about pay and performance hidden. This increases the firm's power in pay negotiations, takes advantage of workers' behavioral bias to be overconfident about their performance and pay, and allows a firm to vary pay based on nonperformance factors like family-and-friends connections, discrimination, and silencing squeaky wheels with grease. When I discussed the hiring process, I suggested that the best way for individuals to deal with the information gaps that exist is to try to close them. It should be clear that the same applies after you get hired. Once you have that great job, you need to figure out what matters, how it is measured, and how to be sure that what you do gets counted.

CHAPTER TWELVE

How People Shop, the Great Recession, and the End of the Soviet Union

Markets and Prices Can Be Challenging, but the End Result Is Positive

One conclusion you might draw from the range of prices and markets we have covered is that consumers can face a pretty challenging time in doing things well in a market economy. In a single eventful day you can be misled by bait-and-switch advertising, have important information hidden from you in buying a computer printer, have your decision-making biases exploited in choosing a cell phone plan, have to deal with an expert repair person who can take advantage with their specialized knowledge, and have to deal with the pervasive information gaps involved in looking for a new job. It is evident that a market system is not an economy for wimps. Americans like to see themselves as independent and tough individuals who can deal with things, so perhaps that's why a market economy seems to fit so well in the United States.

When you consider all these issues, the question inevitably comes to mind whether people in general can actually do a good job at picking and choosing how they spend their money in a market system. Does it all just overwhelm them, or do they in fact do pretty well in figuring it out? As you think about the sheer number of prices and markets there are in an economy, another question comes to mind: If some of those markets and prices matter more than others, what would happen if a critical price was somehow wrong?

How People Shop

As we found earlier, people are burdened by a host of biases that make it hard to shop well. Some of these seem to be hardwired in our brains, like valuing things more highly because we own them, putting noncritical decisions off into the future, and our sense of fairness in relations with others. These biases, however, are only a partial list of the tendencies that researchers have found when they study how people act in buying, selling, and dealing with money. People are susceptible to the particular way goods are offered, for example. If you put healthy food at the start of the line in a cafeteria, people will tend to choose more of it to eat. In an experiment at a business conference, arranging a snack table with sliced apples in front and sliced brownies in back compared to a second table with whole brownies in front and whole apples in back led to the consumption of 84 percent more apples and 30 percent fewer brownies from the "healthy" arrangement. People also look for patterns in the world in order to help them understand what is happening around them. This tendency makes people see patterns where none exist. Most basketball fans believe a player who has made his past three shots is more likely to make his next one, but study after study has shown that in fact the idea of a "hot hand" is a myth. This tendency to see patterns where none exist can be particularly troublesome when people are thinking about investing some of their hard-earned money in the stock market. As we found earlier, people also tend to be overly optimistic about the decisions they make. The vast majority of people believe their marriages will be a success, and many more students believe they are among the top 50 percent in a class than believe they are in the bottom 50 percent.

One of the biases that make economic decisions particularly hard is that we can be overwhelmed by choice. People obviously like choice. They don't choose to wear identical clothes or drive identical cars or buy identical watches. As a result, you might think that the more choice the better. This, however, doesn't appear to be the case. A survey reported in *The Economist* cited case after case where less choice actually made things better for people in making economic decisions. In experiments using jams, coffee, and writing pens, people responded more positively to choices offering fewer rather than more options. Some firms have even reacted to findings like these by reducing their offerings. When a major shampoo brand reduced its choices from twenty-six to fifteen, sales rose by 10 percent. A leading paint brand also reduced its wall colors from 1,000 to 282 because they became convinced that "less is more."

These innate behavioral tendencies make sense because they help us handle all the information and decisions we have to deal with in getting by from day to day. These biases lead to what one study of the issue calls "coarse thinking," another labels "rational inattention," and has been summed up in the economic literature as the "adaptive markets hypothesis." Whatever you call it, lumping similar things together as patterns, picking the first good thing we see presented to us, putting nonessential things off to the future, and shying away from complex choices all help us make decisions rapidly and well enough to get things done. But it is easy to see how these tendencies can get us in trouble when we are dealing with prices and markets. You certainly don't want to get the patterns wrong when you are choosing the ways to invest your savings. Putting off saving for retirement indefinitely because there are always more immediate things that need to be done can create a real crisis at the end of your life. And buying the attractively displayed first thing you see when you walk into a store is probably not going to get you the best deal available.

With this burden of innate biases, it seems that we are doomed to bumble our way through the economy, making mistakes all along the way. In fact, it is clear that people do make many mistakes in dealing with prices and markets. As a recent article on these issues put it, *homo sapiens* is not *homo economicus*, the super-rational decision maker often assumed in economic models. We simply are not like a Deep Blue supercomputer analyzing millions of possible moves in a game of Go when it comes to dealing with prices and markets. It was mistakes that people commonly make when dealing with money that inspired researchers to look for the causes of these errors in the first place. But is the situation a true disaster from the point of view of the normal buyer? If you look at a large group of people and follow them around to see how they buy things, do people shop well?

The answer seems to be that, in fact, they do. Rachel Griffith, Ephraim Leibtag, Andrew Leicester, and Aviv Nevo were able to provide insight into this question from a data set collected in the United Kingdom in the year 2006. They had scanner data covering all food and beverage purchases for 23,877 households in some 5.6 million separate shopping trips. Their focus in the study was in seeing how effective people were in taking advantage of four savings possibilities: buying on sale; buying in bulk; buying generic versus brand names; and shopping at low-price discount stores. These savings opportunities are well known to anyone who does any shopping, and the authors wanted to know if people actually took good advantage of them. Given the data they had, the authors were able to calculate both the potential savings that shoppers could make in each of these categories over the year, and the actual savings they received.

The conclusion of the authors was that people took advantage of all four areas of potential savings at a similar order of magnitude. The mean savings in all four areas combined amounted to over 400 pounds per year (about 700 dollars in 2018 dollars). They also found that the savings differences between households showed patterns that one would expect given their different circumstances. Households with cars and with larger homes, for example, took greater advantage of bulk buying and sales, presumably because they had a better ability to take larger quantities home and store them. Families with children also saved more by using all four possibilities than did families without children. The authors were also able to make some preliminary comparisons with similar data they had collected for the United States. They found that savings from sales and bulk purchases were larger in the United States than in the United Kingdom, apparently because more people had cars and live in larger homes in the United States.

More specific information on the United States, this time focusing on spending by poor households, was provided in another study of scanner data by Christian Broda, Ephraim Leibtag, and David Weinstein. Using 2005 data on the food purchases of 40,000 households, the authors were interested in testing the conventional wisdom that in the United States the poor, because of their lack of mobility and choice, paid higher prices than higher-income households for the goods they bought. Broda, Leibtag, and Weinstein found that tracking actual purchases of households, rather than using surveys of shelf prices or other techniques available in the past, changed the conclusion. They found that, in fact, the poor pay less for the goods they purchase. In their data set, compared to higher-income households, the poor shopped more often at discount stores, and they paid lower prices for the goods they bought in the same retail stores.

Another experiment by the Office of Fair Trading in the United Kingdom came up with similar positive results. The purpose of the study was to see how shoppers responded to five different common pricing strategies: the bait-and-switch; time-limited offers; three-for-two offers where the unit price had to be worked out; sales; and add-on pricing where only part of the price is revealed at first and then extra charges are added. The subjects were 166 students who made buying decisions in a computer game. The buyers did make errors. They made the most significant errors under add-on pricing, followed by time-limited offers, baiting, sales, and three-for-two-type offers. However, under all schemes the buyers made the right decision most of the time. They also clearly learned, as they made better decisions as the experiment went on.

The implication of these studies is good news. It seems that despite all the circumstances we face that can cause us to make mistakes involving prices and markets, people do a pretty good job of shopping. I know that I find it helpful to look at a list of reminders I keep on my smartphone that includes the phrases "Chuck's soda," "diagnosis and remedy," "moats and gaps," "real price ≠ ticket price," and "mind the gap!" The first note is to remind me about how I really want to spend my money by thinking about my friend Chuck's experience buying large drinks at his favorite restaurant. The second helps me organize my thoughts when I deal with experts. The third is a reminder of the ideas of moats to cross and information gaps to fill when I have to deal with issues related to labor markets. The fourth reminds me of the lessons from gift giving, free online services, and pollution that the real price you pay for a good can be quite different from its ticket price, and the fifth reminds me that the answer to many issues in dealing with markets is taking the time to collect more information.

In general, it appears we do a decent job of learning from our experiences with markets and taking advantage of the opportunities we have to save a buck. This probably shouldn't be a surprise, given all the attention you give to getting the most you can out of your income. But it's nice to know that it seems to hold true across large groups of households. We certainly have reason to gripe about this or that in our dealing with everyday prices and markets, but it is encouraging to know that it's not beyond our abilities to do a pretty good job in figuring things out. Ultimately, when you think about it, this should be what you expect. After all, if people in southern California can survive driving the 92 million miles traveled on Los Angeles County roads each day, they can certainly figure out how to deal with the prices and markets they have to cope with when they arrive at their destinations. Taking an even broader view, in his 2016 book *Progress: Ten Reasons to Look Forward to the Future*, Johan Norberg chronicles how the world is a richer, healthier, safer, and more tolerant place than even a few decades earlier, and certainly much of this has been due to the basic success of the economic decisions people make in their daily lives.

The Great Recession and the End of the Soviet Union

The question about whether there are some critical prices in the economy and what would happen if those prices were somehow wrong is about how all the prices and markets we deal with in everyday life work as a whole. It would be comforting to know that when you bring all the thousands of prices and markets together that everything mixes and matches well. Unfortunately, as everyone knows who has lived in an economy like the one in the United States for long, that is not always the case. There are critical prices in the economy, and getting those prices wrong can create problems for the whole system.

The Great Recession of 2007–2009 provides an example. The causes and consequences of the events leading up to and reinforcing the decline have been described in dozens of books and articles. The story is too complex to pick a single cause—even the official government report on the crisis contained three different explanations—but most observers agree that a key factor in causing all the problems was getting a price wrong.

The price that seems to have mattered a lot in leading up to the Great Recession was the price of borrowing to buy a house. Buying a house, of course, is one of those things, like buying a car and paying for college, that almost everyone needs to borrow money in order to do. Before the early 2000s, to get a house loan in the United States required a substantial down payment, proof of ability to repay the loan, and a ceiling placed on borrowing costs as a percentage of your income. These requirements limited the amount of money that people could borrow to buy a house, and this in turn controlled the price of houses. In the early 2000s, however, these restrictions on borrowing pretty much disappeared in the housing market. As a result, borrowing increased, and the prices of houses followed upward.

Using data sources and computer-processing ability not available to study earlier recessions, Atif Mian and Amir Sufi concluded that the easy access to credit in the early 2000s was a primary cause of the Great Recession. The rising housing prices and easy lending terms also caused people who already owned houses to borrow even more by using their houses as collateral, and caused others to start buying houses not to live in but to hold for a short time and then resell to make a quick profit. Mian and Sufi found in their study that existing homeowners increased their borrowing against their homes from 25 to 30 cents for each dollar that the value of their homes rose. They found that most of this money went for home improvements and consumption and not to pay down debt or buy new properties.

The end came, as we know, when house prices started to fall and people in large numbers found they could not make the payments on the loans they had taken out. The final result was a 10 percent national unemployment rate, 25 percent of homeowners owing more for their houses than they could sell them for, and a long, slow recovery. Given all the factors at work creating recessions, maintaining the old standards behind the price of borrowing to buy a house may not have stopped a recession from happening in the United States, but a pretty good case can be made that if we had kept the old lending standards in place we may be calling that event the recession of 2008 (not capitalized) rather than the Great Recession of 2007–2009.

The disaster of 2007–2009, with its foundation in getting a key price wrong in the economy, is not very reassuring. To make matters worse, it can be argued that the collapse of the Soviet Union in the late twentieth century had a lot to do with getting some prices wrong. The prices that appear to have mattered in creating the chronic long-term economic decline of the Soviet Union were input prices, the prices that firms pay for the materials they need for production. According to János Kornai, a Hungarian economist who identified the problem while it was ongoing and before it became fatal, the economic systems of the Soviet Union and its satellite countries had a very different information and incentive system than market economies. The economic systems of the Soviet area were planned-command systems. Goods had prices in these systems that on the surface looked like those in market economies, but in fact planned-command prices were often very different than in market systems.

Kornai found that the prices that consumer-goods buyers faced in planned-command systems were much like the prices that consumers face in market systems. There was not much of a problem here. Consumers had a certain amount of income they earned from their jobs, and they used this income to buy goods provided in the marketplace, just as people do in market economies. Kornai argued that the situation was quite different, however, for firms. Firms in the planned-command economies made their production decisions based on orders from a central planning organization and not based on signals received from their sales in the marketplace. As a result, firms aimed to fulfill orders coming from the directors above them and not from the customers that they served. In Kornai's terms, the firms were motivated by quantity targets and not profit targets.

A consequence of this incentive system was that firms did not worry about profits or losses. Firms paid prices for the materials they bought and received prices for the goods they sold, but these prices were set by the planners and mainly served a bookkeeping purpose. If the firms made a loss, the state budget covered it. If they made a profit, the government took most of it in part to cover the losses of other firms. Firms did not go bankrupt because any shortfall in revenue over cost would be taken care of by the central planners. Kornai said that planned-command firms faced a "soft-budget constraint," as opposed to the hard-budget constraint of bankruptcy faced by market system firms.

According to Kornai, it was this quantity-target/soft-budget constraint pricing that in a fundamental way caused the planned-command economic systems to wind down over time and cease to grow. Because they were ordered to meet planned output targets, firms hoarded and wasted materials. The cost and inefficiency in input markets dragged the system down, and since input markets are fundamental to the very structure of an economic system, the burden became ever greater over time. Planners knew about these problems, of course, and efforts were constantly made to overcome the chronic production inefficiencies, but in the end the remedies were not effective. As a 2017 article on the issue put it, "The Soviets . . . could move resources into the factories, but they could not maintain the efficiency with which they were used."

The fundamental problem with input prices in planned-command systems was that they did not convey the same information that input prices convey in market systems. The information problem showed up explicitly in the innovation record of planned-command economies. According to Marshall Goldman, the Soviet system could keep up with slow-moving technologies but not with the accelerating pace of innovation being generated in post–World War II market systems. The price signals of profit and loss that motivated innovation in market economies did not exist in the planned-command systems.

The importance of information contained in market prices is a point that was made early in the twentieth century by Friedrich von Hayek during a debate over whether planned-command systems could even work. Von Hayek argued that a critical feature of prices in market systems is that they are much more than bookkeeping aids. Market prices are loaded with information. The fact that market prices carry critical information is no surprise to anyone who

lives in a market system. When you have to buy something for your home—
say a gallon of interior latex paint—you take account of the information contained in the prices of different brands of paint without even thinking about
it. Assume that your local hardware store has interior latex priced at $15, $25,
$30, $35, and $70 per gallon. As an experienced consumer in a market sys-
tem, you automatically make some assumptions about the paint based on the
information conveyed by its prices. Unless there is some incredible special
attached to the $15 paint, you are going to assume that the quality is pretty
bad. You will probably assume as well that the gradation from $25 to $35 on
the next three choices also indicates some quality differences, with the more
expensive paint being better in some dimensions that you can inquire about.
The $70 paint you probably expect is a designer brand name that is selling its
name as well as the paint, and you may doubt that the price actually reflects
a significant improvement in quality.

Von Hayek pointed out that the fact that prices carry information like this
is what makes market systems work so well. For a market system to work,
individual consumers and individual firms do not have to know a lot of information. Individual consumers and individual producers just have to know a
few prices, and to know that those prices reflect both the scarcity and the quality of the goods they are choosing among. The key decision makers in market
systems, in other words, do not have to know a great deal about the millions
of details about the economy. In contrast, for a planned-command system to
work the central planners have to know enormous amounts of information.
To do their job well, central planners have to know the alternative technologies that exist to produce all the goods chosen for the economy to produce.
They have to know the amounts of all the resources available for firms to use
in production, including all the minerals, all the labor, all the energy sources,
and everything else. The key decision makers in a planned-command system
have to know a huge amount to make the system work.

Market systems, then, are very efficient in the provision and use of information. The system can work with each consumer and firm—the key decision makers in the system—knowing only the prices that relate to the
particular goods they are interested in. Planned-command systems, on the
other hand, are just the opposite. In order to operate effectively, planners, who
are the key decision makers in planned-command systems, must know a great
deal about many things. In particular, they must know an enormous amount
about the production side of the economy.

In practice, the operation of a quantity-target, soft-budget-constraint incentive system where production prices carry little information worked to slow
economic growth in planned-command economies to a standstill. There was,
of course, much else at work during the second half of the twentieth century
in the contest between planned-command and market systems. The need for
the Soviet Union to keep up with the United States in the arms race and the

need for the Soviet Union to control politically its satellite nations created an enormous financial burden. But the information efficiencies of market systems compared to the production and innovation inefficiencies of command-planned systems played a fundamental role in bringing the planned-command systems to a breaking point.

In effect, the planned-command systems of the twentieth century were a grand economic experiment—played out over decades—that ultimately failed. The failure, however, was relative. Planned-command systems worked; they just did not work as well as market systems. Certainly, anyone who lives in a market system knows that they are not perfect. Prices in market economies, although they convey information efficiently and effectively, do not convey information ideally. Problems with markets abound, as the examples in the previous chapters have made clear. Taking a broad overview, it is apparent that market systems have two great advantages and two great problems.

The two great advantages of market systems are efficiency and innovation. Looking back at János Kornai's comparison of market and planned-command economies, the focus on profit maximization in a context of hard budget constraints forces firms in market systems to use inputs efficiently. Firms aim to produce the kind and quality of goods that consumers want at the least possible cost. This motivation causes firms to conserve their use of inputs and to be constantly on the lookout for new and better ways to produce their goods. As a result, innovation blossoms on both the output and input sides of markets. Where on the input side firms search for new and better ways to produce goods, on the output side they are constantly looking for new and better goods that appeal to consumers. It is not a surprise that Bill Gates became the wealthiest person in the world by creating a company in a market system based on a new innovation.

The great weaknesses of market systems, on the other hand, are insecurity and inequality. The insecurity comes from two inherent characteristics of market systems, their constant change and their tendency to cycle. The fact that firms are always looking for new and better products and for more efficient ways to produce those products creates ceaseless change. Products come and go, as do the ways they are produced. This is positive in many ways, but it has embedded in it the negative result that people who have committed their wealth or their labor to a particular industry can find that their wealth is lost or their labor no longer needed. When firms go bankrupt, the firm, being an abstract legal creation, feels no pain. The investors in that firm and the people who work for it, however, can have their well-being destroyed. This inherent characteristic of market systems is exacerbated by the fact that market systems have an inherent tendency to cycle. Innovations do not occur evenly over time, and people tend to act in concert because they lack complete knowledge about the future. The result is an uneven sequence of rising and falling growth that adds another dimension to insecurity in market systems.

Inequality, the second great negative of market systems, comes from the fact that people earn their incomes in market economies from selling the resources they own to firms that need inputs in production. The distribution of resources owned by individuals is not equal, nor are the prices that markets put on different resources. As a result, people who happen to own resources that are highly valued in the marketplace can do very well indeed. Those who own few or less desired resources may not be able to earn enough to buy the necessities of life.

A second factor creating inequality in market systems is that people can make mistakes in their economic decisions. As we found in our discussions about dealing with experts, negotiating house loans, and reviewing cell phone plans, to do well in a market system requires paying attention. Some people do better than others in making these decisions, and the result is unequal outcomes.

The dual nature of market systems, with their balance of strengths and weaknesses, has been recognized for a long time. As Jerry Muller put it in his 2002 book titled *The Mind and the Market*, "the capitalist market is now and has ever been a morally complex and ambiguous entity. This has long been recognized both by its strongest critics and its subtlest advocates." In the 1940s Joseph Schumpeter came up with probably the best short summary of the working of market systems when he claimed that market economies are systems of "creative destruction." The creative part is based on innovation and efficiency and makes market systems grow and generate wealth. The destruction part comes from insecurity and inequality as individuals are forced to deal with the ceaseless change and regular cycles that are inherent in the system.

The purpose of much economic legislation in market economies is to try to take advantage of the strengths of market systems while controlling or alleviating the weaknesses. Antitrust laws exist to stop firms from taking advantage of the power they may have in their markets. Employment laws about hiring, firing, and promotion exist to promote equality in the treatment of workers who have the very human characteristics of not being identical in the quality and specifics of the labor inputs they sell in the labor market. Social Security, Medicare, food stamps, and other income redistribution programs exist to even out the inequality of individual outcomes in market systems. Environmental laws exist to adjust for the failure of firms to take into account all of the costs incurred in their production of goods and services. Government licenses are required to correct for problems created by asymmetric information between providers and consumers. Legal and court systems are developed to fairly and consistently enforce laws and regulations. The issues in market systems that require some kind of legislation to adjust, correct, prevent, or regulate is a long one.

Government, of course, does not do this work ideally. One of the venerable uses of government going back thousands of years is to use government action to make market outcomes even more unequal. Monopolies can be granted, unreasonable occupational licenses required, incomes taxed, labor forced, and innovation stopped. Economic legislation also tends to focus on narrow immediate effects and not consider broader longer-term consequences. It is depressingly easy to replicate stories about fraud, waste, and inefficiency in government programs. This, however, should not be a surprise. Government making economic decisions, after all, was the problem in the planned-command economies.

Despite all these issues and problems with market systems, there clearly has been a general movement in recent decades for nations across the world to make greater use of markets in dealing with economic decisions. Certainly, the planned-command systems of Eastern Europe have moved in this direction, as, just as clearly, have India and, most spectacularly, China. This general movement has been evident even within market systems. The United Kingdom, beginning under Margaret Thatcher, is perhaps the clearest example, but the United States, starting with the Carter and Reagan administrations, did a great deal to reduce regulations that limit markets. France and Germany moved in the same direction, as have, even more dramatically, Mexico and many other nations in Central and South America. There are exceptions to this general movement—North Korea, Cuba, and Venezuela during the early-to-mid-2000s clearly moved in the direction of less use of market incentives. But the general direction has been clear.

The reason that most of the nations in the world moved toward using more market solutions to their economic problems in recent decades has much to do with the fact that the strengths of market systems outweighed the strengths of planned-command systems. It was not a victory of ideology, however, but of experience. All one had to do was look around the world in the late twentieth century to see that the countries emphasizing market solutions were doing better than planned-command systems. The four tigers of Asia—Singapore, Taiwan, Hong Kong, and South Korea, which developed their economies over thirty years from poverty levels to general well-being—did not have a counterpart in the planned-command world. As John Plender concluded in a 2015 book, weighing all the issues related to market systems, "capitalism is the worst form of economic management, except for all those other forms that have been tried from time to time."

As countries moved toward a greater use of markets to take advantage of their strengths, they had to deal with their weaknesses as well. As they faced these inherent issues, different nations have chosen different solutions. The great planned-command economic experiment of the twentieth century may be over, but the great market-system economic experiment of the twenty-first century is just beginning.

The varied approaches that nations take to resolving the issues inherent in market systems create different versions of market economies. For some nations, the inequality created by market forces is too much to bear. These nations may follow the market model created by Sweden, which has one of the most equal income distributions among rich countries in the world. For other nations, the insecurity created by the creative destruction of market systems will be a focus. Germany and France may be models here, with their emphasis on providing a strong social safety net that protects individuals and families. Other nations may want to preserve values reflected in political systems or state religions and act to constrain market forces that affect political or customary practices and relationships. China and Iran seem to fit here. Others, such as the United States, may value equality of opportunity over equality of results, and create institutions that create this outcome.

As they make these changes, countries constantly modify and revisit what they have done. The sentiment in the United States after the Great Recession of 2007–2009 was certainly different from that in the late 1990s. The events of those ten years convinced many that the freeing up of markets had gone too far, especially in the financial sector, and that a return to older forms of control were necessary. As market economy nations make these changes, both the creative and the destruction parts of "creative destruction" are limited and controlled. The goal in controlling the "creative" part is to channel creativity in particular directions or to stop its encroachment on traditional practices. The goal in controlling the "destruction" part is to protect those hurt by market forces or to limit these effects.

The ways that countries create their own version of market economies involve, to a large degree, influencing market prices. Prices and markets are argued about, controlled, freed, manipulated, praised, and castigated as nations attempt to reap the benefits while limiting the costs of their market systems. As nations go about this process of examining and modifying their economic systems, one thing seems clear. People who are fascinated by prices—their causes, their effects, and their explanations—will have plenty to do in a world where markets and prices are relied on more than ever to guide and make economic decisions.

As we go about our daily life, we don't concern ourselves much with these broader issues about prices and markets. We concentrate instead on dealing with the prices and markets that we come in contact with during the day. In doing this, we are actually playing a central role in making the economy work the way it does. That is, after all, how a market system functions, by individual consumers and producers focusing on the information provided in the prices and markets that immediately affect them.

What this all adds up to is that although there certainly are times when dealing with prices and markets is challenging, the end result is actually encouraging. The fact that most nations in the world are creating different versions of market economies indicates that in practice prices and markets do their job pretty well. The fact that people are good shoppers suggests that people do deal with the prices and markets they face quite effectively. The fact that price patterns are explained by specific structural and behavioral factors means that market results are understandable. It is not too difficult for us to understand, for example, why the price for candy bars varies between the vending machine down the hall and the grocery warehouse across town, why our favorite superstar got a contract for that amazing sum of the money, or how an asymmetry in information between buyers and sellers can affect the price of our used car. Since these patterns we see in prices and markets are understandable, they can be improved and people can figure out how to do better for themselves. The Pension Reform Act of 2006, after all, did change how people plan for their retirement, mortgage education classes do improve the mortgages people negotiate, and using her cell phone to search for comparison prices does allow my daughter to haggle for better prices. The prices and markets that surround us are the best way that people have ever been able to come up with to solve the practical problems of producing and distributing goods, and although the daily effort of dealing with them might make us hesitate in our enthusiasm from time to time, the challenges are well worth taking on.

References

Introduction

Anagol, Santosh, Vimal Balasubramaniam, and Tarun Ramadorai. "Endowment Effects in the Field: Evidence from India's IPO Lotteries." August 27, 2017. https://ssrn.com/abstract=2702555.

Autor, David H., David Dorn, and Gordon H. Hanson. "The China Shock: Learning from Labor-Market Adjustment to Large Changes in Trade." *Annual Review of Economics* 8 (October 2016): 205–40.

"The Consensus Crumbles." *The Economist*, July 2, 2016, 67.

Diamond, Jared. *The World Until Yesterday*. New York: Penguin Books, 2012, 60.

"The Economics of Self-Storage." *The Economist*, August 18, 2012, 60.

"GDP per Capita (Current US$)." China. data.worldbank.org.

"Get Off of My Cloud." *The Economist*, January 14, 2017, 69.

Graeber, David. *Debt: The First 5,000 Years*. New York: Melville House, 2012, 39.

Horwitz, Tony. *Blue Latitudes: Boldly Going Where Captain Cook Has Gone Before*. New York: Holt, 2002, 189.

"The Impact of Free Trade." *The Economist*, July 30, 2016, 43.

"On the Origin of Specie." *The Economist*, August 18, 2012, 68.

"Rise of the Supergrid." *The Economist*, January 14, 2017, 71.

Smith, Adam. *An Inquiry into the Nature and Causes of the Wealth of Nations*. Dunwoody, GA: Norman S. Berg, 1976, 5.

Thomas, Lewis. *The Lives of a Cell: Notes of a Biology Watcher*. New York: Viking Press, 1974.

Chapter 1

Akerlof, George. "The Market for 'Lemons': Quality Uncertainty and the Market Mechanism." *Quarterly Journal of Economics* 84 (August 1970): 488–500.

Badenhausen, Kurt. "Major League Baseball's Highest Paid Players for 2018." *Forbes,* April 11, 2018. https://www.forbes.com/kurtbadenhausen/2018.

Becker, Gary S. "A Theory of the Allocation of Time." *Economic Journal* 75 (September 1965): 493–517.

"Brands Are Finding It Hard to Adapt to an Age of Skepticism." *The Economist*, February 1, 2014, 58.

Busse, Meghan, Jorge Silva-Risso, and Florian Zettelmeyer. "$1,000 Cash Back: The Pass-Through of Auto Manufacturer Promotions." *American Economic Review* 96 (September 2006): 1253–70.

Haller, Sonja. "YouTube's Top Earner Is a 7-Year-Old Who Made $22 Million Playing with Toys." *USA Today,* December 5, 2018. https://www.usatoday.com/story/life/allthemoms/2018/12/05/youtube-top-earner-7-year-old-made-22-million-playing-toys/2206508002/.

"Information Asymmetry." *The Economist*, July 23, 2016, 55–56.

Krome, Charles. "Car Depreciation: How Much Value Will a New Car Lose?" *Carfax*, November 9, 2018. https://www.carfax.com/blog/car-depreciation.

Lewis, Greg. "Car Depreciation: How Much Have You Lost?" *Trusted Choice,* May 14, 2018. https://www.trustedchoice.com/insurance-articles/wheels-wings-motors/car-depreciation/.

Marks, Tod. "Tips on How to Bargain and Save Money: 89 Percent of Those Who Haggled Were Rewarded at Least Once." http://w.w.w.consumerreports.org/cro/magazine/2013/08/how-to-bargain/index.htm.

Rosen, Sherwin. "The Economics of Superstars." *American Economic Review* 71 (December 1981): 845–58.

Stigler, George J. "The Economics of Information." *Journal of Political Economy* 69 (June 1961): 213–25.

"Taming the Titans." *The Economist*, January 20, 2018, 11.

Willcox, James K. "Get the Most TV for Your Money." *Consumer Reports* 83 (December 2018): 27.

Chapter 2

"All Prizes in Economic Sciences." https://www.nobelprize.org/nobel_prizes/economic-sciences/laureates.

Grubb, Michael D. "Selling to Overconfident Consumers." *American Economic Review* 99 (December 2009): 1770–1807.

"In Praise of Procrastination." *The Economist*, July 7, 2012, 64.

Johnson, Dominic. *God Is Watching You: How the Fear of God Makes Us Human.* Oxford: Oxford University Press, 2015.

"The Last Diamond Mine." *The Economist*, February 25, 2017, 50–52.

Pope, Devin, and Maurice Schweitzer. "Is Tiger Woods Loss Averse? Persistent Bias in the Face of Experience, Competition, and High Stakes." *American Economic Review* 101 (February 2011): 129–57.

Raihani, N. J., and K. McAuliffe. "Human Punishment Is Motivated by Inequity Aversion, Not a Desire for Reciprocity." *Biology Letters* 8 (July 2012): 802–804.

"Richard Thaler Wins the Nobel Prize for Economic Sciences." *The Economist*, October 14, 2017, 68.

Scott, Frank, and Aaron Yelowitz. "Pricing Anomalies in the Market for Diamonds: Evidence of Conformist Behavior." *Economic Inquiry* 48 (April 2010): 353–68.

Shermer, Michael. "It Doesn't Add Up: When It Comes to Money, People Are Irrational. Evolution Accounts for a Lot of It." *Los Angeles Times*, January 13, 2008.

Sloman, Steven, and Philip Fernbach. *The Knowledge Illusion: Why We Never Think Alone*. New York: Riverhead Books, 2017.

Thaler, Richard H., and Cass R. Sunstein. *Nudge: Improving Decisions about Health, Wealth, and Happiness*. London: Penguin Books, 2009, 31–35, 105–17.

"When Nudge Comes to Shove." *The Economist*, May 20, 2017, 51–52.

Chapter 3

Bikhchandani, Sushi, David Hirshleifer, and Ivo Welch. "Learning from the Behavior of Others: Conformity, Fads, and Informational Cascades." *Journal of Economic Perspectives* 12 (Summer 1998): 151–70.

"Brands Are Finding It Hard to Adapt to an Age of Skepticism." *The Economist*, February 1, 2014, 58.

Bronnenberg, Bart J., Sanjay Dhar, and Jean-Pierre H. Dubé. "Brand History, Geography, and the Persistence of Brand Shares." *Journal of Political Economy* 117 (February 2009): 87–115.

"The Case for Brands." *The Economist*, September 8, 2001, 11.

"Google a Photoshopped Hoover." *The Economist*, September 9, 2017, 80.

Hendricks, Ken, and Alan Sorenson. "Information and the Skewness of Music Sales." *Journal of Political Economy* 117 (April 2009): 324–69.

Hirshleifer, David. "The Blind Leading the Blind: Social Influence, Fads, and Informational Cascades." In *The New Economics of Human Behavior*, edited by Mariano Tommasi and Kathryn Ierulli. Cambridge, MA: Cambridge University Press, 1995, 188–215.

"I've Got You Labelled." *The Economist*, March 31, 2011. https://www.economist.com/science-and-technology/2011/03/31/ive-got-you-labelled.

Mercier, Hugo, and Dan Sperber. *The Enigma of Reason: A New Theory of Human Understanding*. Cambridge, MA: Harvard University Press, 2017.

"The New Manufacturing Footprint." *The Economist*, January 14, 2017, 60.

Pashigian, B. Peter, and Brian Bowen. "Why Are Products Sold on Sale? Explanations of Pricing Regularities." *Quarterly Journal of Economics* 106 (November 1991): 1015–38.

Pashigian, B. Peter, Brian Bowen, and Eric Gould. "Fashion, Styling, and the Within-Season Decline in Automobile Prices." *Journal of Law and Economics* 38 (October 1995): 281–309.

Thaler, Richard H., and Cass R. Sunstein. *Nudge: Improving Decisions about Health, Wealth, and Happiness*. London: Penguin Books, 2009, 53–60.

Thompson, Derek. *Hit Makers: The Science of Popularity in an Age of Distraction*. London: Penguin Press, 2017.

van de Rijt, Arnout, Soong Moon Kang, Michael Restivo, and Akshay Patil. "Field Experiments of Success-Breeds-Success Dynamics." *Proceedings of the National Academy of Sciences,* April 28, 2014. https://doi.org/10.1073/pnas.1316836111.

"Yes, Ten Million People Can Be Wrong." *The Economist*, February 19, 1994, 81.

Young, H. Peyton. "The Economics of Convention." *Journal of Economic Perspectives* 10 (Spring 1996): 105–22.

Chapter 4

"Battling Bots." *The Economist*, January 7, 2017, 24.

Courty, Pascal. "Some Economics of Ticket Resale." *Journal of Economic Perspectives* 17 (Spring 2003): 85–97.

"The Economics of Gifts." *The Economist,* June 30, 2018, 68.

"The Gift of Last Resort?" *Consumer Reports*, December 2015, 44–45.

"Have Yourself a Dismal Christmas." *The Economist*, December 23, 2017, 92.

List, John A. "Does Market Experience Eliminate Market Anamolies? The Case of Exogenous Market Experience." *American Economic Review* 101 (May 2011): 313–17.

List, John A., and Jason Shogren. "The Deadweight Loss of Christmas: Comment." *American Economic Review* 88 (December 1998): 1350–55.

Offenberg, Jennifer Pate. "Markets: Gift Cards." *Journal of Economic Perspectives* 21 (Spring 2007): 227–38.

Smolensky, Eugene, Leanna Stiefel, Maria Schmundt, and Robert Plotnick. "In-Kind Transfers and the Size Distribution of Income." In *Improving Measures of Economic Well-Being*, edited by Marilyn Moon and Eugene Smolensky. New York: Academic Press, 1977, 131–53.

Solnick, Sara J., and David Hemenway. "The Deadweight Loss of Christmas: Comment." *American Economic Review* 86 (December 1996): 1299–1305.

"Trading Gift Cards for Cash." *Consumer Reports*, March 2011, 11.

Waldfogel, Joel. "The Deadweight Loss of Christmas." *American Economic Review* 83 (December 1993): 1328–36.

Waldfogel, Joel. "The Deadweight Loss of Christmas: Reply." *American Economic Review* 86 (December 1996): 1306–1308.

Waldfogel, Joel. "Gifts, Cash, and Stigma." *Economic Inquiry* 40 (July 2002): 415–27.

Yang, Adelle X., and Oleg Urminsky. "The Smile-Seeking Hypothesis: How Immediate Affective Reactions Motivate and Reward Gift-Giving." *Psychological Science* 29 (August 2018): 1221–33.

Chapter 5

"Believing Is Seeing." *The Economist*, August 27, 2016, 58.

"Counterfeiting and Piracy." *The Economist*, April 23, 2016, 51–52.

"Craft in Mexico." *The Economist*, August 25, 2018, 28.

Ezrachi, Ariel, and Maurice E. Stucke. "Two Artificial Neural Networks Meet in an Online Hub and Change the Future." *Oxford Legal Studies Research Paper No. 24/2017,* July 1, 2017. https://ssn.com/abstract=2949434.

Higgins, Richard S., and Paul H. Rubin. "Counterfeit Goods." *Journal of Law and Economics* 29 (October 1986): 211–30.

Lazear, Edward P. "Bait and Switch." *Journal of Political Economy* 103 (August 1995): 813–30.

"Price-Match Guarantees Prevent Rather Than Provoke Price Wars." *The Economist*, February 14, 2015, 68.

Qian, Yi. "Impacts of Entry by Counterfeiters." *Quarterly Journal of Economics* CXXIII (November 2008): 1577–1609.

Samuels, Alana. "Wanna Buy Some Knockoff Jeans?" *Los Angeles Times*, September 6, 2008.

Waldman, Don E., and Elizabeth J. Jensen. *Industrial Organization: Theory and Practice*, 3rd ed. Boston: Pearson Addison Wesley, 2007, 311–13.

Walker, Mandy. "When Are Sales Too Good to Be True?" *Consumer Reports* 83 (December 2018): 40–45.

Chapter 6

Agarwal, Sumit, Gene Amromin, Itzhak Ben-David, Souphala Chomsisengphet, and Douglas D. Evanoff. "Learning to Cope: Voluntary Financial Education and Loan Performance during a Housing Crisis." *American Economic Review* 100 (May 2010): 495–500.

Ausubel, Lawrence M. "The Failure of Competition in the Credit Card Market." *American Economic Review* 81 (March 1991): 50–81.

Balafoutas, Loukas, Rudolf Kerschbamer, and Matthias Sutter. "Second-Degree Moral Hazard in a Real-World Credence Goods Market." *The Economic Journal* 127 (February 2017): 1–18.

"Beating Back Cable Fees." *Consumer Reports*, February 2019, 7.

Bohr, Peter. "Perplexed by Prices." *Westways*, September 2013, 64.

Calem, Paul S., and Loretta J. Mester. "Consumer Behavior and the Stickiness of Credit-Card Interest Rates." *American Economic Review* 85 (December 1995): 1327–36.

Dulleck, Uwe, and Rudolf Kerschbamer. "On Doctors, Mechanics, and Computer Specialists: The Economics of Credence Goods." *Journal of Economic Literature* XLIV (March 2006): 5–42.

Gabaix, Xavier, and David Laibson. "Shrouded Attributes, Consumer Myopia, and Information Suppression in Competitive Markets." *Quarterly Journal of Economics* 121 (May 2006): 505–40.

Lacko, James M., and Janis K. Pappalardo. "The Failure and Promise of Mandated Consumer Mortgage Disclosures: Evidence from Qualitative Interviews and a Controlled Experiment with Mortgage Borrowers." *American Economic Review* 100 (May 2010): 516–21.

Levitt, Steven D., and Stephen J. Dubner. *Freakonomics,* rev. ed. New York: Morrow, 2006, 65–69.

Levitt, Steven D., and Stephen J. Dubner. *Super Freakonomics.* New York: Morrow, 2009, 39.

Monticello, Mike. "Can You Trust Your Auto Repair Shop?" *Consumer Reports* 84 (February 2019): 52–57.

O'Sullivan, Arthur, and Steven M. Sheffrin, *Economics: Principles and Tools,* 4th ed. Upper Saddle River, NJ: Pearson Prentice Hall, 2005, 305–307.

"Payment-Card Fees." *The Economist,* October 15, 2016, 71.

Rysman, Marc. "The Economics of Two-Sided Markets." *Journal of Economic Perspectives* 23 (Summer 2009): 125–43.

"Shuffle and Deal." *The Economist,* October 28, 2017, 67–68.

Stango, Victor. "Pricing with Consumer Switching Costs: Evidence from the Credit Card Market." *Journal of Industrial Economics* 50 (December 2002): 475–92.

Woodward, Susan E., and Robert E. Hall. "Consumer Confusion in the Mortgage Market: Evidence of Less Than a Perfectly Transparent and Competitive Market." *American Economic Review* 100 (May 2010): 511–15.

Chapter 7

"The Books Business." *The Economist,* September 10, 2011, 69–70.

"Crony Capitalism." *The Economist,* April 15, 2017, 59.

"The Economics of Digital Music Favour Streaming." *The Economist,* May 7, 2016, 73.

Ehrenberg, Ronald G. "American Higher Education in Transition." *Journal of Economic Perspectives* 26 (Winter 2012): 193–216.

"Fashion Retailing." *The Economist,* September 10, 2016, 56.

"The Film Business." *The Economist,* July 14, 2018, 57.

"Float of a Celestial Jukebox." *The Economist,* January 13, 2018, 55–56.

Gallery 72. Via mailchimpapp.net. Email to author. December 11, 2018.

Goolsbee, Austan, and Chad Syverson. "How Do Incumbents Respond to the Threat of Entry? Evidence from the Major Airlines." *Quarterly Journal of Economics* CXIII (November 2008): 1611–33.

Heilbroner, Robert, and Aaron Singer. *The Economic Transformation of America: 1600 to the Present,* 4th ed. Fort Worth, TX: Harcourt Brace, 1999, 94–95.

Kestenbaum, Richard. "Jeff Bezos Says 'Amazon Is Not Too Big to Fail.' He's Right." *Forbes,* November 16, 2018. https://www.forbes.com/sites/richardkesten baum/2018/11/16/amazon-is-not-too-big-to-fail-bezos/#35c657a11626.

"The Last Pinball Machine." *The Economist,* March 11, 2000, 72.

"The Microeconomics of Uber's Attempt to Revolutionize Taxi Markets." *The Economist,* March 29, 2014, 80.

Miller, Roger LeRoy, Daniel K. Benjamin, and Douglass C. North. *The Economics of Public Issues,* 14th ed. Boston: Pearson Addison Wesley, 2005, 103–109.

Miller, Roger LeRoy, Daniel K. Benjamin, and Douglass C. North. *The Economics of Public Issues*, 15th ed. Boston: Pearson Addison Wesley, 2008, 119–23.

Minzesheimer, Bob. "Hope for Small Bookstores?" *USA Today,* February 10, 2011.

"The New Manufacturing Footprint." *The Economist*, January 14, 2017, 60.

"Online Shopping and Business." *The Economist*, November 19, 2016, 48–49.

Pilkington, Mark. *Retail Therapy: Why the Retail Industry Is Broken—And What Can Be Done to Fix It.* London: Bloomsbury, 2019.

"Retailing." *The Economist*, November 10, 2018, 65.

"Road Haulage." *The Economist*, March 5, 2016, 60–62.

"Shops to Showrooms." *The Economist*, March 12, 2016, 65.

"Small-Town Newspapers." *The Economist*, June 23, 2018, 27.

"Tears for Sears." *The Economist*, October 20, 2018, 59.

Teixeira, Thales S., and Greg Piechota. *Unlocking the Customer Value Chain: How Decoupling Drives Consumer Disruption.* New York: Currency, 2019.

"The Travel Business." *The Economist*, August 25, 2012, 49–51.

"Turning the Page." *The Economist*, May 5, 2012, 65–66.

Waldman, Don E., and Elizabeth J. Jensen. *Industrial Organization: Theory and Practice*, 3rd ed. Boston: Pearson Addison Wesley, 2007, 150–53, 335–51.

"The Year of the Incumbent." *The Economist*, January 6, 2018, 49.

Chapter 8

Appel, Timothy. "Japan Finds Loophole in Whaling Ban." *Christian Science Monitor*, April 15, 1987.

Barrios, John M., Yael V. Hochberg, and Hanyi Livia Yi. "The Cost of Convenience: Ridesharing and Traffic Fatalities." November 20, 2018. https://www.ssrn.com/ abstract=3271975.

Cousteau, Jacques. *Whales*. New York: Abrams, 1986.

Eckard, E. Woodrow. "The 'Law of One Price' in 1901." *Economic Enquiry* 42 (January 2004): 101–10.

Gill, Lisa L. "How to Pay Less for Your Meds." *Consumer Reports* 84 (January 2019): 46–50.

"Jumbo Cartels." *The Economist*, February 11, 2017, 45.

Pashigian, B. Peter, and Eric D. Gould. "Internalizing Externalities: The Pricing of Space in Shopping Malls." *Journal of Law and Economics* 41 (April 1998): 115–42.

Schaller, Bruce. *The New Automobility: Lyft, Uber and the Future of American Cities*. Brooklyn, NY: Schaller Consulting, July 25, 2018. www.schallerconsult.com.

Sorensen, Alan T. "Equilibrium Price Dispersion in Retail Markets for Prescription Drugs." *Journal of Political Economy* 108 (October 2000): 833–50.

Tregarthen, Timothy. *Microeconomics*. New York: Worth, 1996, 104, 110.

"Ubernomics." *The Economist*, November 3, 2018, 70–71.

Chapter 9

"Brussels to End Pricing Probe into Disneyland Paris." *FT Weekend*, International, April 17, 2016, 3.

Harless, David W., and George E. Hoffer. "Do Women Pay More for New Vehicles? Evidence from Transaction Price Data." *American Economic Review* 92 (March 2002): 270–79.

"How to Tame the Tech Titans." *The Economist*, January 20, 2018, 11.

Kaplan, Dean, and John A. List. "Does Price Matter in Charitable Giving? Evidence from a Large-Scale Natural Field Experiment." *American Economic Review* 97 (December 2007): 1774–93.

Keynes, John Maynard. *The General Theory of Employment Interest and Money*. New York: Harcourt, Brace & World, 1936, 161–62.

"Loyalty Schemes." *The Economist*, September 9, 2017, 64–65.

Marshall, Alfred. *Principles of Economics*. London: Macmillan, 1890.

McKenzie, Richard B. *Why Popcorn Costs So Much at the Movies and Other Pricing Puzzles*. New York: Copernicus Books, 2008, 60, 101–10.

"A Row over Printer Cartridges." *The Economist*, October 1, 2016, 63.

Streitfeld, David. "Amazon Mystery: Pricing of Books." *Los Angeles Times*, January 2, 2007.

Chapter 10

Akerlof, George A., and Janet Yellen. *Efficiency Wage Models of the Labor Market*. Cambridge: Cambridge University Press, 1986.

Azar, José A., Ioana Marinescu, and Marshall I. Steinbaum. "Labor Market Concentration." *NBER Working Paper No. 24147*, December 2017.

Azar, José A., Ionna Marinescu, Marshall I. Steinbaum, and Bledi Taska. "Concentration in US Labor Markets: Evidence from Online Vacancy Data." *NBER Working Paper No. 24395*, March 2018, revised August 2018.

"Better, Stronger, Faster." *The Economist*, March 3, 2018, 70.

Carter, Thomas J. "Efficiency Wages: Employment versus Welfare." *Southern Economic Journal* 62 (July 1995): 116–26.

"Competition." *The Economist*, November 17, 2018, 4.

Cottle, Michelle. "The Onerous, Arbitrary, Unaccountable World of Occupational Licensing." *The Atlantic*, August 13, 2017. https://www.theatlantic.com /politics/archive/2017/08/trump-obama-occupational-licensing/536619/.

Diamond, Michael L. "State Attorneys General Want to Know More about Fast-Food 'No Poach' and Noncompete Agreements." *USA Today Network*, July 9, 2018. https://www.usatoday.com/story/money/nation-now/2018/07 /09/fast-food-no-poach-agreements/769560002/.

Fairris, David, and Lee J. Alston. "Wages and the Intensity of Labor Effort: Efficiency Wages versus Compensating Payments." *Southern Economic Journal* 61 (July 1994): 149–61.

Frank, Robert H., and Philip J. Cook. *The Winner-Take-All Society.* New York: Free Press, 1995.

Furman, Jason, and Laura Guiliano. "New Data Show That Roughly One-Quarter of U.S. Workers Hold an Occupational License." U.S. Council of Economic Advisers. June 17, 2016. www.whitehouse.gov/blog/2016/06/17/new-data -show-roughly-one-quarter-us-workers-hold-occupational-license.

Guiso, Luigi, Ferdinando Monte, Paola Sapienza, and Luigi Zingales. "Culture, Gender, and Math." *Science* 320 (May 30, 2008): 1164–65.

Kahn, Lawrence M. "The Sports Business as a Labor Market Laboratory." *Journal of Economic Perspectives* 14 (Summer 2000): 75–94.

Kleiner, Morris M., and Alan B. Krueger. "Analyzing the Extent and Influence of Occupational Licensing on the Labor Market." *Journal of Labor Economics* 31 (April 2013): S173–S202.

Konezal, Mike, and Marshall Steinbaum. "Declining Entrepreneurship, Labor Mobility, and Business Dynamism: A Demand-Side Approach." Roosevelt Institute. July 21, 2016. rooseveltinstitute.org/declining.

"Licensing Laws." *The Economist*, October 28, 2017, 31.

"Making Pay Work." *The Economist*, May 25, 2013, 76.

Mehta, Shailendra Raj. "The Law of One Price and a Theory of the Firm: A Ricardian Perspective on Interindustry Wages." *RAND Journal of Economics* 29 (Spring 1998): 137–56.

"Migrant Workers in the UAE." *The Economist*, April 9, 2016, 74.

"Migration in the Gulf." *The Economist*, September 10, 2016, 39.

Milgrom, Paul, and John Roberts. *Economics, Organization and Management.* Englewood Cliffs, NJ: Prentice Hall, 1992.

Murphy, Kevin M., Andrei Shleifer, and Robert W. Vishny. "The Allocation of Talent: Implications for Growth." *Quarterly Journal of Economics* 106 (May 1991): 503–30.

Naidu, Suresh, Yaw Nyarko, and Shing-Yi Wang. "Worker Mobility in a Global Labor Market." National Bureau of Economic Research. NBER Working Paper No. 20388, August 2014. nber.org/papers/w20388.

"Occupation Licensing Blunts Competition." *The Economist*, February 17, 2018, 25–26.

Posner, Eric A., Glen Weyl, and Suresh Naidu. "Antitrust Remedies for Labor Market Power." *Harvard Business Review* 132 (December 2018): 536–601.

Raff, Daniel M. G., and Lawrence H. Summers. "Did Henry Ford Pay Efficiency Wages?" *Journal of Labor Economics* 5, Part 2 (October 1987): 557–86.

"Recruitment and Equality." *The Economist*, August 13, 2016, 56.

Shapiro, Carl, and Joseph E. Stiglitz. "Equilibrium Unemployment as a Worker Discipline Device." *American Economic Review* 74 (June 1984): 433–44.

"Shifting Shifts." *The Economist*, December 8, 2018, 30.

Sommers, Paul M., and Noel Quinton. "Pay and Performance in Major League Baseball: The Case of the First Family of Free Agents." *The Journal of Human Resources* 17 (Summer 1982): 426–36.

"The Terrible Threat of Unlicensed Interior Decorators." *The Economist*, May 14, 2011, 84.

Thoreau, Henry David. *Walden*. New York: Norton, 1951, 45.

"Too Much of a Good Thing." *The Economist*, March 26, 2016, 23–24, 26, 28.

United States. Senate. Committee on the Judiciary. Subcommittee on Antitrust, Competition Policy and Consumer Rights. *License to Compete: Occupational Licensing and the State Action Doctrine*. Hearing. February 2, 2016.

"Workers Benefit When Firms Must Compete Aggressively for Them." *The Economist*, July 30, 2016, 62.

Chapter 11

"Academic Sexism: Purblind Prejudice." *The Economist*, September 23, 2017, 74.

Akerlof, George. "The Economics of Caste and of the Rat Race and Other Woeful Tales." *Quarterly Journal of Economics* 90 (November 1976): 599–617.

"Beauty and Success." *The Economist*, December 22, 2007, 53–54.

"The Evolution of Beauty." *The Economist*, November 16, 2013, 81–82.

Flaherty, Colleen. "Anonymous Comments, Unmasked Bias." *Inside Higher Ed*, August 21, 2017. into.ai/blog/news-stories/anonymous-comments-unmasked-bias.

Goldin, Claudia, and Cecilia Rouse. "Orchestrating Impartiality: The Impact of 'Blind' Auditions on Female Musicians." *American Economic Review* 90 (September 2000): 715–41.

Hamermesh, Daniel S. *Beauty Pays: Why Attractive People Are More Successful*. Princeton, NJ: Princeton University Press, 2011.

Hamermesh, Daniel S., and Jeff. E. Biddle. "Beauty and the Labor Market." *American Economic Review* 84 (December 1994): 1174–94.

Hengel, Erin. "Publishing While Female: Are Women Held to Higher Standards? Evidence from Peer Review." March 2019. www.erinhengel.com/research.

"Labour Markets." *The Economist*, September 29, 2018, 29–30.

Landers, Renée M., James B. Rebitzer, and Lowell J. Taylor. "Rat Race Redux: Adverse Selection in the Determination of Work Hours in Law Firms." *American Economic Review* 86 (June 1996): 329–48.

Perez, Caroline Criado. *Invisible Women: Exposing Data Bias in a World Designed for Men*. London: Chatto & Windus, 2019.

Prokosch, Mark, Ronald Yeo, and Geoffrey Miller. "Intelligence Tests with Higher G-Loadings Show Higher Correlation with Body Symmetry." *Intelligence* 33 (March–April 2005): 203–13.

Rhode, Deborah. *The Beauty Bias: The Injustice of Appearance in Life and Law*. Oxford: Oxford University Press, 2010.

Rhodes, Gillian, and Leslie Zebrowitz, eds. *Facial Attractiveness: Evolutionary, Cognitive, and Social Perspectives*. Santa Barbara, CA: Praeger, 2001.

"Study Thyself: Sexism in Economics." *The Economist*, January 12, 2019, 63.

Wolfers, Justin. "Evidence of a Toxic Environment for Women in Economics." *The New York Times,* August 18, 2017. https://www.nytimes.com/2017/08/18/upshot/evidence-of-a-toxic-environment-for-women-in-economics.html.

Wu, Alice H. "Gender Stereotyping in Academia: Evidence from Economics Job Market Rumors Forum." August 2017. calwomenofecon.weebly.com/uploads/9/6/1/0/96100906/wu_ejmr_paper.pdf.

Chapter 12

"America's Financial Crisis Commission." *The Economist*, January 29, 2011, 72.

"The Big Squeeze." *The Economist*, November 11, 2017, 68.

Broda, Christian, Ephraim Leibtag, and David E. Weinstein. "The Role of Prices in Measuring the Poor's Living Standards." *Journal of Economic Perspectives* 23 (Spring 2009): 77–97.

"Expanded State Ownership Is a Risky Solution to Economic Ills." *The Economist,* June 17, 2017, 70.

Goldman, Marshall I. *What Went Wrong with Perestroika.* New York: Norton, 1992, 36.

Griffith, Rachel, Ephraim Leibtag, Andrew Leicester, and Aviv Nevo. "Consumer Shopping Behavior: How Much Do Consumers Save?" *Journal of Economic Perspectives* 23 (Spring 2009): 99–120.

Hansen, Pella Guldborg. "iNudgeYou Does Health Nudge Experiment on Buffet Arrangement." iNudgeYou.com, February 11, 2013.

"How Kids Are Adapting to a Cashless Culture." *PBS NewsHour,* March 7, 2019. https://www.pbs.org/newshour/show/how-kids-are-adapting-to-a-cashless-culture.

Kornai, János. *Economics of Shortage.* Amsterdam: North-Holland, 1980.

Kornai, János, Eric Maskin, and Gérard Roland. "Understanding the Soft Budget Constraint." *Journal of Economic Literature* XLI (December 2003): 1095–1136.

Landreth, Harry, and David C. Colander. *History of Economic Thought*, 4th ed. Boston: Houghton Mifflin, 2002, 494–95.

"The Lives of the Parties." *The Economist*, December 15, 2018, 73.

Lo, Andrew. *Adaptive Markets: Financial Evolution at the Speed of Thought.* Princeton, NJ: Princeton University Press, 2017.

Mian, Atif, and Amir Sufi. *House of Debt: How They (and You) Caused the Great Recession, and How We Can Prevent It from Happening Again.* Chicago: University of Chicago Press, 2014.

"Miles of Public Roads." Los Angeles Almanac. laalmanac.com/transport/tr01.htm.

Mullainathan, Sendhil, Joshua Schwartzstein, and Andrei Shleifer. "Coarse Thinking and Persuasion." *Quarterly Journal of Economics* CXXIII (May 2008): 577–619.

Muller, Jerry Z. *The Mind and the Market: Capitalism in Modern European Thought.* New York: Knopf, 2002, xiv.

Norberg, Johan. *Progress: Ten Reasons to Look Forward to the Future.* London: Oneworld, 2016.

"The Paradox of Choice." *The Economist*, February 11, 2017, 12.

Plender, John. *Capitalism: Money, Morals and Markets.* London: Biteback, 2015.

Schumpeter, Joseph. *Capitalism, Socialism, and Democracy,* 3rd ed. New York: Harper and Brothers, 1950, 83.

Sims, Christopher. "Rational Inattention: Beyond the Linear-Quadratic Case." *American Economic Review* 96 (May 2006): 158–63.

Thaler, Richard H., and Cass R. Sunstein. *Nudge: Improving Decisions about Health, Wealth, and Happiness.* London: Penguin Books, 2009, 1–3.

Tooze, Adam. *Crashed: How a Decade of Financial Crisis Changed the World.* New York: Viking, 2018.

"The Tyranny of Choice." *The Economist*, December 18, 2010, 123–25.

"What's the Alternative?" *The Economist*, August 15, 2015, 75.

Index

British supermarket price-match policy, 55
Broda, Christian, 127
Bronnenberg, Bart, 36
Buffalo, 86
Buffet, Warren, 110
Busse, Meghan, 9, 15, 18
Buying more at a lower price, 90–101; Alfred Marshall, 90–91; Chuck's soda, 94; college grants, 99–101; consumer advice, 94–95; Halloween candy, 91; law of demand, 92; price discrimination, 95–99; reason for, 91; sensitivity to price, 91; soft drinks, 92–95; start high and lower price over time, 92–93; start low and raise price over time, 93–94
Buying studies, 127

Calem, Paul, 65–66
Callback studies, 115
Candy bars: as a price-plus good 12–13; time to purchase, 12; variation in price, 11–12
Carbon tax, 82
Career choice, 112–113; discrimination, 113; explanatory factors, 112–113; growth effects, 113; relation to superstars, 113
Cattlemen's associations, 85–86
Cell phone plans, 24–25; consumer advice, 25; overconfidence, 25; pricing, 24; status quo bias, 25
Checklist for high-paid jobs, 104, 108–109
China: beauty wage premium, 116; counterfeiting, 52; gross national product, 3; market system, 134–135; prices, 1
Choice bias, 125
Christmas gifts, 40–41
Chuck's soda, 94, 127
Classroom demonstrations: coffee mug values, 4–5; coin toss game,

23; trading yard sale items, 2; ultimatum game, 22–23
Closely comparable products, 77
Coarse thinking, 125
Coca-Cola Company, 98
Coffee mug classroom demonstration, 4–5
Coin toss game, 23
College grants, 99–101; consumer advice, 100–101; early admission, 99–100; matching gifts, 101; negotiable prices, 100; price discrimination, 99–100
College tuition, 73–75; competition, 73–74; consumer advice, 75; differences between buyers, 73–74; features, 73; government regulation, 74; information gaps, 73; prices, 73; technological change, 75; value of a college degree, 74
Competition for workers, 105–106; concentration in labor markets, 106; *kafala* system, 106; Major League Baseball, 105–106; noncompete clauses, 106; trends, 106; wage effects, 106
Competitive markets, 19; college tuition, 73; trends 76
Computer printers, 98
Concentration in labor markets, 106
Consumer advice: Angie's List, 29; bait-and-switch, 50; brands, 37–38; buying more at a lower price, 94–95; cell phone plans, 25; college grants, 100–101; college tuition, 75; *Consumer Reports*, 10, 29, 36–37, 47, 59, 60; credit cards, 67; diamonds, 27; endangered species, 86; expert advice, 59–60; externalities, 83–84; fads, 35; fashion goods, 32; 401(k)s, 22; fundamental issues involved, 7, 135–136; gift cards, 47; haggling, 10; Halloween candy, 92; hidden fees, 65; high-paid jobs,